"Michal Shapira's latest book is a refreshing, original and revealing exploration of one of Freud's most intriguing, misunderstood and neglected case studies."

Elizabeth Grosz, author of *Jacques Lacan: A Feminist Introduction* (Routledge, 1990)

"Michal Shapira's brilliant, close analysis of Sigmund Freud's final published case study, his 1920 'The Psychogenesis of a Case of Homosexuality in a Woman,' has been the least examined but perhaps one of the most relevant of his cases for our time... A book of true importance today."

Sander L. Gilman, author of *Freud, Race, and Gender* (Princeton University Press, 1993)

Sigmund Freud and his Patient Margarethe Csonka

This book provides a historical analysis of one of Sigmund Freud's least-studied cases, published in 1920 as "The Psychogenesis of a Case of Homosexuality in a Woman."

Scholars of sexuality often focus on Freud's writings on male homosexuality, disregarding his views on homosexual women. This book serves as a corrective, renewing and reinvigorating interest in Freud, and demonstrating that his views on sexuality are as relevant today as ever. Part I introduces the case and explores Freud's attitudes towards lesbianism, radical among his medical colleagues in the early twentieth century. It also puts Margarethe Csonka, the patient, at its center. Michal Shapira considers Freud's only treatment of a "female homosexual" and assesses Csonka's background life before and after the encounter. Part II expands the case beyond the scientific-medical purview of the times and looks at the new opportunities afforded to women and assimilated Jews through growing equality and the modernization of urban life in 1920s Vienna.

This book places Csonka's case within the broader context of medical and psychological texts, Freud's own writings, Jewish and queer history, and modern Vienna's urban and art history. *Sigmund Freud and his Patient Margarethe Csonka* will be of great interest to psychoanalysts in practice and in training, and to readers interested in the history of gender and sexuality, feminism, modern European and urban history, the history of psychoanalysis, science and medicine, and the history of ideas.

Michal Shapira, PhD, is Associate Professor in the History Department at Tel Aviv University, Israel. She previously taught at Barnard College, Columbia University and Amherst College, USA.

History of Psychoanalysis

Series Editor: Peter L. Rudnytsky

This series seeks to present outstanding new books that illuminate any aspect of the history of psychoanalysis from its earliest days to the present, and to reintroduce classic texts to contemporary readers.

Other titles in the series:

For further information about this series please visit https://www.routledge.com/The-History-of-Psychoanalysis-Series/book-series/KARNHIPSY

Sigmund Freud and his Patient Margarethe Csonka

A Case of Homosexuality in a Woman in Modern Vienna

Michal Shapira

R Routledge
Taylor & Francis Group

LONDON AND NEW YORK

Designed cover images: Freud image is: © Freud Museum London
Margarethe Csonka image is: The Sigmund Freud Museum

First published 2024
by Routledge
4 Park Square, Milton Park, Abingdon, Oxon OX14 4RN

and by Routledge
605 Third Avenue, New York, NY 10158

Routledge is an imprint of the Taylor & Francis Group, an informa business

© 2024 Michal Shapira

British Library Cataloguing in Publication Data
A catalogue record for this book is available from the British Library

ISBN: 978-1-032-40349-6 (hbk)
ISBN: 978-1-032-40348-9 (pbk)
ISBN: 978-1-003-35266-2 (ebk)

DOI: 10.4324/9781003352662

Typeset in Times New Roman
by Taylor & Francis Books

This book is dedicated to my wife Jessica Levin who is my love and a miracle in the world

Contents

Figures

Acknowledgements

I would like to thank Susannah Frearson, the editor at Routledge for her kind help throughout the different stages of the book, Jana Craddock, Alison Phillips, Dominic Corti and Peter Rudnytsky, editor of the History of Psychoanalysis series. Thanks also go to Carol Seigel and Tom Derose at the Freud Museum London, and to Elana Shapira and Daniela Finzi at the Sigmund Freud Museum in Vienna for their invaluable help.

The participants of the Columbia University International History Workshop and Susan Pedersen offered comments on previous related work on women in the psychological realm that were of great help to me in writing this book. The work of Elizabeth Grosz made me think better about the topics discussed here and she was the first scholar I discussed them with to great effect. Lesley Marks provided fine editorial skills and excellent suggestions and additions, especially in the final stages. Some of the research was generously supported by the Israel Science Foundation (grant no. 1344/21).

My grateful thanks go to my former students for their important input: Dean Teplitsky was the smartest research assistant with the finest attention to detail; he helped to locate the documents for the individual family members discussed in the book. Gil Engelstein provided wise comments on the manuscript, and Yasmine Segol, Vered Shimshi and Eliya Amsalen offered their wonderful help as well.

I thank my kind and loyal friends who listened to me discussing this project at length: Eyal Shpringer, Yifat Shpringer, Ronny Regev, Reut Harari, On Barak, Roy Flechner, Noam Maggor, Galia Limor-Sagiv, Jonathan Shulman, Assaf Shir, Yaelle Kayam, Itamar Alcalay, Izabel Barak, Snyveli Levin, Jill Payne, Smadar Zilber, Tariq Jaffer, Daniel Ussishkin, Jon Marcus, Gary Ross, Jonathan Cohen, Brian Kates, Nurit Levin, Zohar Bar Kama and Naama Cohen-Hanegbi. Special thanks to Doron Halutz for his excellent comments. Bonnie G. Smith provided ongoing support and wisdom as always and I am truly grateful for her friendship. The same thanks for their kind support over many years also go to Billie Melman and Moshe Sluhovsky.

An article from the book is published with changes in a different format as "'Not Unsympathetic': Freud's Lesser-Known 1920 Case of the Female Homosexuality of Margarethe Csonka," *Journal of the History of Sexuality*, 32, no. 3 (2023), 340–374.

The book is written in memory of my Jewish relatives on my late grandmother's side. My grandmother, Esther Shapira (née Falkon), was born in Thessaloniki, Greece, and passed away in 2018 in Tel Aviv, Israel, at the age of 94. Her Thessaloniki relatives lived there until 1943, but were murdered during the Holocaust. They included David, Gedalia, Bouena (Tova née Cohen), Desi, Serina, Sylvia, Palumba Yona, Yitzhak from the Falkon family as well as Yitzhak, Aron, Binyamin ('Bino') and Dvora ('Dudun') from the Filo family, and Mazaltov (née Falkon) and Yaacov from the Russo family. The book is also written in memory of my grandparents Yitzhak Shapira and Lea and Arie Fenster and in memory of Saul, Henry and Selina Fenster, Rivka Shaul, and Boaz Neumann.

I give my loving thanks to my family, especially my parents Tzippi and Gadi Shapira, my sister Mor, and my nieces and nephew Maya and Nahar Shaul, Emily and Sylvie Levin, as well as other family members including Shoshana, Nat and Ely Levin, Carolyn Weiss, Yuval Shaul, Tali Shapira, Ada and Ariel Fenster, Hanni and Yossi Shapira, and Alon Burg. And last, but by no means least, I thank Jessica Levin, the love of my life. She makes every day full of laughter and joy and working on the book was so much easier with her encouragement, endless support and sweetness. I am so grateful for our love together—it is a cosmic power!

Introduction

Sigmund Freud's case studies, dedicated to the analysis of the histories of individual patients, are among his most well-known and well-researched writings. The literature on Freud usually notes the cases of Dora (1905), Little Hans (1909), Rat Man (1909), Dr. Daniel Paul Schreber (1911), and Wolf Man (1918). However, his sixth and last case, written in 1920 and dedicated to the homosexuality of a young woman, has received much less attention among psychoanalytic scholars, and undoubtedly even less among historians. The theorist Diana Fuss noted that it "may well be Freud's most overlooked case study; certainly, compared to the volume of criticism generated by the Dora case."[1]

Titled "The Psychogenesis of a Case of Homosexuality in a Woman,"[2] it is often omitted from what are considered "Freud's cases," even though this four-month-long treatment of a young woman who fell in love with a woman ten years older than herself was the only explicit instance of "female homosexuality" that Freud analyzed.[3] Such scholarly neglect is perhaps due to a combination of reasons—not one of which stands alone. First, the analysis was short and incomplete, and it was terminated by Freud. Second, Freud did not mention the patient's name or give her a memorable pseudonym as he had with the more famous cases. Third, it was mostly his later, interwar writings on female sexuality that sparked so much debate and possibly obscured this early case of female homosexuality.[4] Indeed, to this we should add that although several analytic articles on female homosexuality were written in the interwar period, they are seldom discussed.[5] Fourth, the patient was not diagnosed as neurotic, and her childhood was not explored in great depth. Fifth, this case signals a process of moving away from the case study towards writing beyond this genre.[6] Sixth and finally, although there were exceptions, the radical attitude towards homosexuality evident in this case was

DOI: 10.4324/9781003352662-1

generally not continued into the period between the 1940s and the 1970s by the many psychoanalysts who turned to more conservative and homophobic views.[7]

The 1920 publication is indeed Freud's only major case history in which the patient is not given a fictitious name, and thus is not afforded the status of a fully drawn character; Freud simply called her "the girl," or *das Mädchen* in German (although she was eighteen when he met her). What we know about this girl, observed the theorist Teresa de Lauretis, is "what he tells us, what she says is in answer to his questions; even her indifference is a sign of *his* feeling rejected, unrecognized, irrelevant."[8] The historical identity of the patient has remained unknown until recently, and was not recognized in the few publications that refer to the case.

However, a new biography, translated from German into English in 2019, has finally exposed the patient's real name, Margarethe Csonka (and her married name, Trautenegg), to English readers. It uncovers her life story spanning most of the twentieth century (1900–1999) in ways that have not received the attention of historians of psychoanalysis or of sexuality. The biography reveals information about this young female patient, her family, and her loves, as well as about Jewish life in Vienna.[9] Historically contextualizing these facts allows me as a historian to craft an alternative narrative, from the point of view of the patient and her background. And it is productive to analyze historically this narrative vis-à-vis the one offered by Freud, which I will also put in context with other prevailing conventional attitudes towards homosexuality in general, and female homosexuality in particular. Freud wrestled with the antisemitic and homophobic ideas of the time, though they permeated his (and Csonka's) views of sexuality.

Historians of sexuality repeatedly focus on Freud's writings on male homosexuality, largely omitting the study of his views on female homosexuality.[10] Freud's complex views in this regard fluctuate between the sexual conventionalism of his time and the relative radicalism for which he is better remembered in relation to male homosexuality. There is a persistent, unresolved tension in his texts between seeing homosexuality as a fixation at an early stage of development on the way to mature heterosexuality on one hand, yet not seeing deviations as necessarily being pathologies on the other. Or, as philosopher Elizabeth Grosz frames it, there is "a tension in Freud's writings between acceptance of the teleology of heterosexual copulation and reproduction, and the perpetual undermining of the naturalness or inevitability of this sexual teleology through his understanding of the constitutive power of the deviations or vicissitudes of sexual aims, objects, and sources of erotic pleasures."[11]

The feminist writers who did refer to Freud's 1920 paper often viewed it mostly as a conservative text in which a misogynist, phallocentric Freud clashed with a young female homosexual patient in ways that led to the analysis's failure and early termination. Thus, scholar Ronnie C. Lesser and others claim that it was the phallo- and heterocentric conventional Freud that dominated the 1920 case "with his heavy-handed, disparaging treatment of the patient and his advancement of a pathological model to explain her lesbianism."[12] Although the case certainly places female sexual development within Oedipal, phallocentric, theoretical models, I would like to stress in contrast that if we read the text within the context of the time, Freud's other writings, and other medical works and ideas, and historicize the theory, it seems to present a much more radical Freud than these feminist readings suggest.[13] In fact, the 1920 case served as a building block in Freud's thinking about homosexuality, and led him to a less judgmental view—at times unequivocally less so than the views of others of his time. Indeed, as early as 1905, in his "Three Essays on the Theory of Sexuality," Freud saw homosexuality as an aberration or deviation in sexual object choice rather than as illness or degeneracy. The 1920 text and his direct encounter with the young woman led him to be even more open, adopting an almost neutral position as he offered a non-pathological stance in his attitude towards homosexuality (in effect opening up future, alternative conceptions beyond the heterosexual telos).

Freud began his 1920 essay by stating that homosexuality in women, though no less common than in men, had been ignored by the law and neglected by psychoanalytic research.[14] Indeed, in most European countries and cities in the early twentieth century, only male homosexuality was criminalized in law.[15] This was not the case in Vienna where women could also be prosecuted under Paragraphs 129b and 130 of the Austrian criminal code. Freud, of course, wrote papers on women before 1920, in which he mostly dealt with hysteria. However, as he developed his model of the Oedipus complex and his 1905 ideas on sexuality, during the interwar period Freud began to focus more closely on the question of female sexuality in his subsequent, highly controversial papers on this topic.[16] Also usually ignored was the fact that the 1920 text on female homosexuality was part of Freud's exploration of femininity, and that female homosexuality was constitutive of his formulations.[17] In what follows, I highlight why we should pay more attention to this paper and see it as part of the history of sexuality; and why, with the revealed details about the young woman in modern Vienna and its assimilated Jewish life, we can gain entirely new insights about the context of the 1920 paper and this patient's world beyond the scientific discourse.[18]

Thus, the overarching goal of this book is to historically situate both Freud and his young female patient within the flourishing medical and cultural-social life of urban Vienna during the early twentieth century. I argue that looking at their narratives in the context of the changing urban, social, and ethnic-religious realities and prevailing medical attitudes of the interwar period will reveal what enabled different ways of thinking and being vis-à-vis same-sex love, and what visions of female same-sex desire emerged at the time. Such an all-encompassing investigation will contribute more broadly to the history of sexuality by illuminating the diverse medical and non-medical ways of understanding and framing homosexual female desire in interwar Vienna.

The first part of this book analyzes Freud's text methodologically and historically in order to carefully situate his 1920 views within the circumstances both of his own writings and the broader sexological and medical debates of the time. This enables me to examine the Freud that Margarethe Csonka met as a young female patient. Freud positioned himself as more radical on the topic of homosexuality than his rivals the sexologists, as he pitted his ideas against theirs in a dichotomous manner. However, new historical studies recently argue that we should think of Freud's medical contemporaries in a more nuanced way.[19] Using this revisionist scholarship will help to reveal his ideas as perhaps less unique or exceptional among all the prevailing complex thinking.[20] Nevertheless, I will clarify where Freud was indeed innovative and how he advanced the discussion on female homosexuality in ways that also historically reveal that he was certainly more radical than later feminists suggested.

The second part of the book juxtaposes Freud's narrative with that of Margarethe Csonka who rejected the language of *scientia sexualis* and experienced same-sex love outside the scientific-medical purview. I will suggest that beyond drawing on models of heterosexual romantic love (explicated in the first part of the book), she effectively utilized other resources as she took advantage of new opportunities that had opened up to women and assimilated Jews through emancipation and the modernization of urban life. Vienna and its dazzling new, modern architecture and culture was an active agent in her affair. The city was very much part of this love story set against the background of Jewish life in the early twentieth century during a shift between increasing gender and ethnic equality and rising antisemitism. Thus, I will argue that it was not only the medical and psychoanalytic discourses that were the source of new ways of being for women, female homosexuals, and Jews; changes in urban development, planning and architecture, trains, the construction of wide streets, new and modern apartment buildings, phone booths, and more, also played a role. In addition, new trends and new rights in the age of mass politics stimulated and enabled new expressions of female same-sex love.

Using the rich trajectory of this encounter between Freud and Csonka, a doctor and a patient engaged in dialogue and resistance, the analysis of both parts of the book will provide a much more nuanced understanding of the different ways in which female same-sex desire was described at the time.[21] Indeed, I will show that Csonka was not just a passive recipient of medical ideas, but rather she was an active subject forging her persona against a backdrop of those city settings that were opening up to her. The conclusion will point to how this meeting of minds in the racist and homophobic realities of the time give us a better grasp of lesbian identity through medical and non-medical concepts, and thereby contribute to a better understanding of the history of female sexuality.

Thus, the book is a revealing historical study of the female queer past in the modern city of Vienna. Focusing on one of Sigmund Freud's least studied cases, it offers a broad view of modern changes in the political, medical, artistic, and architectural spheres, and of battles over the treatment of sexual and ethnic minorities. The case of Csonka also offers a rare window into the world of a person typically ignored by historians as I assess Csonka's assimilated Jewish life before and after the encounters with her doctor and her beloved, and follow the same-sex love and cultural-social life of the young woman patient and her clash of minds with Freud. The book, I hope, rewrites our understanding of the queer, urban, and psychoanalytic past and can also place the current battle for minority rights within the context of a longer history.

Notes

1 Only a few short feminist studies texts dealt with the case. Another edited collection is the exception to this relatively critical neglect. Fuss too notes that the 1920 paper "has received surprisingly little attention." For these

works, and the reference for Fuss, see Diana Fuss, "Fallen Woman: The Psychogenesis of a Case of Homosexuality in a Woman," in *That Obscure Subject of Desire: Freud's Female Homosexual Revisited*, eds. Ronnie C. Lesser and Erica Schoenberg (New York: Routledge, 1999), 73n8; Luce Irigaray, "Commodities Among Themselves," in *This Sex Which Is Not One*, trans. Catherine Porter (Ithaca, NY: Cornell University Press, 1985); Mandy Merck, "The Train of Thought in Freud's 'Case of Homosexuality in a Woman,'" m/f 11–12 (1986): 35–46; Judith A. Roof, "Freud Reads Lesbians: The Male Homosexual Imperative," *Arizona Quarterly* 46, no. 1 (Spring 1990): 17–26; Diane Hamer, "Significant Others: Lesbians and Psychoanalytic Theory," *Feminist Review* 34 (Spring 1990): 134–151; Mary Jacobus, "Russian Tactics: Freud's 'Case of Homosexuality in a Woman,'" in *First Things: Reading the Maternal Imaginary* (New York: Routledge, 1995). Pointing to his blind spots and inconsistencies, the key theoretical attempt to reconsider Freud's ideas on lesbianism is Teresa de Lauretis, *The Practice of Love: Lesbian Sexuality and Perverse Desire* (Bloomington: Indiana University Press, 1994). Her book tried to go beyond a Freudian model of lesbian desire based on masculinity complex and the pre-Oedipal fixation on the mother. It aimed to leave aside the normative Oedipal narrative and articulate instead a model of perverse desire. See the critical questions raised on such an attempt by Elizabeth Grosz, *Space, Time and Perversion* (New York: Routledge, 1995), 155–172. Cf. also the theoretical discussion of the idea of a lesbian phallus and her critical return to Freud's essay on narcissism in Judith Butler, *Bodies that Matter: On the Discursive Limits of Sex* (New York: Routledge, 1993), 57–91. The main historical reference to the case is an article in which a section is dedicated to it: Birgit Lang and Katie Sutton, "The Queer Cases of Psychoanalysis: Rethinking the Scientific Study of Homosexuality, 1890s–1920s," *German History* 34, no. 3 (September 2016): 419–444. See also Lisa Appignanesi and John Forrester, *Freud's Women* (New York: Other Press, 2001).

2 Sigmund Freud, "The Psychogenesis of a Case of Homosexuality in a Woman," *The Standard Edition of the Complete Psychological Works of Sigmund Freud*, ed. J. Strachey (London: Hogarth Press, 1920), vol. 18, 145–172. From here on, *The Standard Edition* is referred to as *SE* with the volume number, date and page number(s) only.

3 If we put aside the homosexuality of Dora, which I discuss below. In the 1920 case, the therapy was conducted during a period when Freud's daughter, Anna, then aged twenty-four (and possibly homosexual), was also in analysis with him. See Sophie de Mijolla-Mellor, "The Psychogenesis of a Case of Homosexuality in a Woman," *International Dictionary of Psychoanalysis Online*. Freud also published the case with this title, including the words "Female Homosexuality" instead of "Homosexuality in a Woman": Sigmund Freud, "The Psychogenesis of a Case of Female Homosexuality," *International Journal of Psychoanalysis* 1, no. 2 (1920): 125–149. As we shall see, in his writings he discussed homosexuality as a position and an object choice rather than as an identity, hence perhaps making the title "Homosexuality in a Woman" in the *SE* the more accurate one.

4 For a recent treatment of this debate, see Michal Shapira, "A Case for a 'Middle-Way Career,' in the History of Psychology: The Work of

Pioneering Psychoanalyst Marjorie Brierley in Early 20th Century Britain," *History of Psychology* 24, no. 1 (2021): 55–76.
5 Michal Shapira, "Psychoanalytic Debates of Female Homosexuality in the Interwar Period," (forthcoming). See also Michal Shapira, "Criticizing Phallocentrism in Interwar Britain: Psychoanalyst Sylvia M. Payne's Kleinian Challenge to Freud," *Modern Intellectual History* (2021): 1–24. See Ernest Jones, "The Early Development of Female Sexuality," *International Journal of Psycho-Analysis* 8 (1927): 459–472; Helene Deutsch, "On Female Homosexuality," *Psychoanalytic Quarterly* 1 (1932): 484–510; Joan Riviere, "Womanliness as Masquerade," *International Journal of Psychoanalysis* 10 (1929): 303–313.
6 Lang and Sutton, "The Queer Cases," 437–438. The authors also speculate that Freud's relative neglect of his patient's early life was also due to the broader lack of interest among psychoanalysts in female sexuality until it was developed during the interwar period, mostly by female analysts. This does not include Jung's Elektra complex, with which Freud disagreed. See 439.
7 For a detailed discussion, see Michal Shapira, *The War Inside: Psychoanalysis, Total War, and the Making of the Democratic Self in Postwar Britain* (New York: Cambridge University Press, 2013), chaps. 5 and 6; Dagmar Herzog, *Cold War Freud: Psychoanalysis in an Age of Catastrophes* (Cambridge: Cambridge University Press, 2016), chap. 2, 56–86. As Herzog writes, "One of the many mysteries surrounding the broad popular success of psychoanalysis in the United States in the first two postwar decades involves the fierce persistence with which analysts insisted on denigrating homosexuality, especially male homosexuality, and the passion they poured into explicating a particular version of femininity, which they insisted must involve sexual responsiveness to men, but on very specifically circumscribed terms," 56.
8 Teresa de Lauretis, "Letter to an Unknown Woman," in Lesser and Schoenberg, *That Obscure Subject of Desire*, 38–39; emphasis in the original.
9 Ines Rieder and Diana Voigt, eds., *The Story of Sidonie C.: Freud's Famous "Case of Female Homosexuality,"* trans. Jill Hannum and Ines Rieder (Budapest: Helena History Press, 2019). It was first published in German in 2000.
10 See S. Flanders, F. Ladame, A. Carlsberg, P. Heymanns, D. Naziri, and D. Panitz, "On the Subject of Homosexuality: What Freud Said," *International Journal of Psychoanalysis* 97, no. 3 (2016): 933–950.
11 Grosz, *Space*, 160.
12 Ronnie C. Lesser, "Introduction," in Lesser and Schoenberg, *That Obscure Subject of Desire*, 6.
13 See also Lang and Sutton, "The Queer Cases of Psychoanalysis."
14 Freud, "The Psychogenesis," 147.
15 Florence Tamagne, *History of Homosexuality in Europe: Berlin, London, Paris 1919–1939* (New York: Algora Publishing, 2003).
16 Editor's Note to Freud, "The Psychogenesis," 146; and see Shapira, "A Case for a 'Middle-Way Career.'"
17 Sophie de Mijolla-Mellor argued that the text "could be considered as the starting point for a development in Freud's study of femininity." Mijolla-Mellor, "The Psychogenesis of a Case."

18 The text includes innovations in topics such as technique of analysis, transference, resistance, dreams, suicide, the differences between male and female homosexuality, and more. See Mijolla-Mellor, "The Psychogenesis of a Case," in which she concisely distinguishes the clinical, epistemological, and technical aspects of Freud's paper.

19 See, for example, Harry Oosterhuis, "Sexual Modernity in the Works of Richard von Krafft-Ebing and Albert Moll," *Medical History* 56, no. 2 (April 2012): 133–155, and the contents of this entire issue of the journal.

20 See H. Oosterhuis, "Freud, and Albert Moll: How Kindred Spirits Became Bitter Foes," *History of Psychiatry* 31, no. 3 (2020): 294–310.

21 In similar ways perhaps, scholars researched Ida Bauer (Dora), Bertha Pappenheim (Anna O), and other patients' lives to understand hysteria among other issues, as well as these patients' multifaceted meetings with Freud. See, for example, C. Bernheim and C. Kahane, eds., *In Dora's Case: Freud-Hysteria-Feminism* (New York: Columbia University Press, 1990); Daniel Boyarin, *Unheroic Conduct: The Rise of Heterosexuality and the Invention of the Jewish Man* (Berkeley: University of California Press, 1997), 313–360; Anat Tzur-Mahalel, *Reading Freud's Patients: Memoir, Narrative, and the Analysand* (London and New York: Routledge, 2020); Anat Tzur Mahalel, "The Wolf Man's Glückshaube: Rereading Sergei Pankejeff's Memoir," *Journal of the American Psychoanalytic Association* 67, no. 5 (2019): 789–813; Anat Tzur-Mahalel, "'Are We Dead': Time in H.D.'s Dialogue with Freud," *International Journal of Psychoanalysis* 102, no. 2 (2021): 297–314.

Part I: Freud, the Medical Discourse, and Female Homosexuality

Background to the 1920 Case History

Psychoanalysis's Reinvention of the Case History Genre

Psychoanalysis presented a new model in the medico-sexological writing genre of the fin-de-siècle case study, for which historian John Forrester coined the term "thinking in cases."[1] In their writings, the founding generation of sexologists such as the German-Austrian psychiatrist Richard von Krafft-Ebing (1840–1902), the British physician Havelock Ellis (1859–1939), and the German psychiatrist Albert Moll (1862–1939) presented cases as autobiographical accounts of patients in a rather straightforward, interpretative manner that could be understood as both pathologizing them, yet gradually also giving them a voice (this tension and complexity are discussed further below in greater detail).[2] In contrast, to advance scientific knowledge and theoretical formulations, Freud looked at the patients' personal accounts as the starting point for reflection, subjecting their voices more directly to a re-evaluation, constantly challenging and problematizing what they said and subverting the opposition between what is considered normal and perverse.[3] As psychoanalytic sessions were based on the idea of unconscious repression and the ability to gain a better knowledge of the self, the psychoanalysts' starting point was to reassess the positioning and presentation of the patients' accounts of themselves in ways that the sexologists did not. Unlike the sexologists who were interested in collecting a large number of cases and were focused on quantity, Freud was keen on selectively using exemplary cases through which to develop and expound his theories.[4] As Forrester explains, "Freud has never betrayed any interest whatsoever in statistical knowledge," whereas sexology and experimental psychology were imbued with statistical methodologies.[5] Indeed, psychoanalysis developed a new method of scientific

DOI: 10.4324/9781003352662-2

reasoning for the case history that involved thinking from the most specific, unique, and peculiar facts that are part of the individual's life and persona, to telling a life public—that is, making it general and scientific.[6] Focusing in depth on the individuality, childhood, primal relationships, fantasies, and inner creations rather than presenting numerous life stories in a statistical manner, Freud challenged the sexological model for dealing with homosexuality. Whereas the sexologists wrote a single paragraph or a few pages about their patients, Freud would dedicate numerous pages to his case studies. Clarifying and illustrating in great detail, he described his theories, methodologies, dream analyses, transference analyses, and how past and present existed together and separately in his patients' lives. These were some of the goals of "writing in cases"—to train readers to think in the psychoanalytic mode, or to "speak Freudian."[7] There is a key tension in his psychoanalytic theory writings as Freud is using a "normative drive" to show how the erotic life of every individual conforms to the exemplar model of the Oedipus story, but at the same time he is also trying and promising to account for "the divergences, the detours, the idiosyncrasies of the individual's life."[8]

Indeed, Sigmund Freud's long case histories about his patients Dora (1905),[9] the Rat Man (1909),[10] Little Hans (1909),[11] Daniel Paul Schreber (1911),[12] and the Wolf Man (1918)[13] are key texts of psychoanalysis and the focus of constant and intense fascination and criticism. Despite the attention they received, historian Anne Sealey reminds us that the genre of writing long cases was in fact short-lived. It was developed mostly towards the end of the nineteenth century, then discarded by the 1920s, almost taking with it the short case history as well. Freud continuously chose to use this genre to illustrate his scientific reasoning and his therapy methods to those readers who were becoming familiar with his basic concepts. He, and other theorists who espoused different versions of the unconscious mind, found that this genre served them well in relating and exemplifying their ways of thinking through psychological rather than physical theories of the mental predicaments of modern Europeans. Psychoanalysts borrowed from the genre of the medical history, which was also being rearticulated at the time. By recounting the full details of a case, Freud was able to convey to his readers the unusual and counterintuitive elements of his theories. This was a living reflection of how he thought in the clinic, and an invitation into his practice. The case history provided him with the perfect framework to articulate and epitomize the way he thought and reached his unexpected conclusions; it made them comprehensible to an ever-growing audience.[14]

Speaking more broadly, we should remember that the articulation of case studies was fundamental to the development of the professional discourse of psychiatry outside of medicine in the nineteenth century. At the turn of the twentieth century, the medical case history in the therapeutic disciplines became more consistent in response to the standardization of scientific journal articles and the pressures of professionalization. Yet this change was not uniform: narrative writing, persuasive arguments, and trained judgments were also seen as important in the making of science. The psychoanalytic case history was developed amid these changes at a time when the discipline itself was emerging. Sealey argues that the long case history was part of the very development and professionalization of psychoanalysis and served as an exemplar in this new discipline. Freud's cases histories can be seen more as hybrid texts that borrowed from empiricist thinking and from the emerging case-based reasoning in the human sciences (which were influenced by methods derived from the natural sciences) at the turn of the twentieth century. The case history was a template that Freud used both to reflect on the assumptions of the medical community or his general audience, and to challenge them using information about individual patients' lives. At the same time, he made his theories and their associated mental conditions comprehensible and plausible, with their own hidden logic. He and his followers only loosely used the commonly accepted medical categories of diagnosis, treatment, and outcome or cure. The focus for Freud was on theory and treatment techniques.[15]

Freud's professional history was rooted in laboratory science and psychiatry at medical school in Vienna where he had witnessed the disciplinary shifts in the formulation of the case history. Thus, he utilized the German laboratory- and lecture-based study, and the empirical experience of the French neurologist Jean-Martin Charcot's Tuesday lessons, to develop his own peculiar ways of presenting his ideas within the case study genre. The fact that early on new psychoanalysts were educated by him via training analyses or lectures must have also contributed to the attraction of case histories as examples for teaching how to think psychoanalytically, and all that this entailed. Within the discipline of psychiatry, case histories usually served either to provide evidence or to present certain forms of disease. Freud used the case histories mostly to illustrate how a disorder could function in a single individual. However, being grounded in the changes involved in the professionalization of psychiatry, he also diverged from case histories and focused instead on discussing the assumptions of psychoanalysis that were at odds with contemporary science.[16]

Even the very form of Freud's case histories supported their theoretical purpose. As Sealey argues, Freud expressed his theoretical commitments in the cases through four formal departures from the shorter case history. He exaggerated these features even compared to many of his contemporaries who wrote long case histories. The first departure is the overall structure. Freud "abandoned the thematic presentation in the traditional case history, and even the traditional chronological order of the case history, to focus on a narrative that more or less corresponded to the order of treatment." The second difference inhered in the amount of detail in the patient's history. Such a thorough exploration "reflected his theory of the etiology of disease, and the mingling of that narrative with its treatment, which also reflects the commitments of psychoanalysis." The third was expressed in Freud's choice to present himself in the case history both as author and protagonist, in contrast to many other case histories that masked the author. Finally, Freud's case histories avoided pathology reports in favor of long-term follow-ups, with the goal of judging the case history's contents.[17] All but the last appeared in the case history of 1920 on female homosexuality.

Perhaps part of the attraction of the psychoanalytic case histories, even until today, lies in their narrative format which extends beyond standard medical writing. Freud used the case histories to explain his diagnosis and method of treatment by turning to powerful narrative writing and combining history-taking and treatment. As Sealey writes, "it was a double narrative—a narrative of the patient's history embedded in a narrative of treatment."[18] Freud's detective-like attention to minute occurrences that would later be revealed as chief causes of mental disorders allowed him to elaborate and exhibit his new theories of childhood and sexuality, and to connect clinical material, techniques, and fresh ideas to great effect. Part of the appeal of his writings (or that which repelled his critics) was his request to be judged primarily on his reasoning and the logic of his theories, as opposed to his contemporaries who hoped to be assessed on the basis of statistical or laboratory measures.[19]

Freud relied on his patients' contributions and their words more than did his medical contemporaries; it was the material from which he formed his narratives, though he seldom took the patient's own narrative at face value. The particularities of his patients and their lives were important but were seen as a platform for developing or winning theoretical arguments, or illustrating the validity of his claims. Freud's focus was continuously on theory and therapy rather than on data and statistics. However, once the theoretical basis of

psychoanalysis was established, the form of writing in long cases—
with exceptions that continue into the present day—was largely abandoned. The 1920 case was the last of Freud's case histories, and we
now turn to its particularities.[20]

Freud began the 1920 case study by describing in detail what led to
the treatment.[21] His patient was "a beautiful and clever girl of eighteen, belonging to a family of good standing," who worried her parents with the "devoted adoration" with which she pursued a "society
lady," about ten years older than herself.[22] The young woman's infatuation had swallowed up all her interests. Despite "her lady's" aristocratic background, the girl's parents believed she was "nothing but a
cocotte [sic]"[23]—an upper-class woman making a living from prostitution. The passionate girl, however, tried to seize every opportunity
to be with her beloved, including waiting for hours outside her door or
at a tram-halt.[24] Freud recounted that one such occasion, when the
father saw his daughter in the lady's company and passed them by
with an angry glance, led to a suicide attempt by his daughter who
threw herself onto the suburban railway line which ran close by. The
girl survived and in fact her situation improved: "she found it easier to
get her own way than before. Her parents did not dare oppose so
much determination in her, and the lady, who until then had received
her advances coldly, was moved by such unmistakable proof of serious
passion and began to treat her in a more friendly manner."[25] After six
months' recovery it was the girl's parents, not the girl herself, who
sought psychoanalytic advice for their daughter when Vienna was still
recovering from the upheaval of the First World War.[26]

Freud accepted the girl as a patient and described her parents' attitudes. When the father, tender yet stern, learned of his daughter's
homosexual tendencies, he was enraged and tried to suppress them with
threats. He viewed her either as vicious, or through the lens of some
then-popular medico-sexological views that labelled her as degenerate
or mentally afflicted. Her homosexuality aroused deep bitterness in him,
and he was determined to combat it either with the help of psychoanalysis or, if that failed, by a marriage that would hopefully stifle his
daughter's "unnatural" tendencies. The mother, however, was a young-
ish woman who did not take her daughter's infatuation so tragically—
she even enjoyed it—she was mainly worried about the harm to the
girl's reputation. Additionally, the mother, whom Freud described as
neurotic, was harsh towards her daughter yet over-indulgent to her
three sons, the youngest of whom was not yet three.[27]

As a psychoanalyst, Freud focused on the young woman's sexuality,
concluding that nothing seemed remarkable in her history and no

sexual traumas were recorded. Indeed, Freud believed that she had gone through the developmental stages that befitted his model of sexuality. In childhood, he argued, the girl had passed through the normal attitude characteristic of the feminine Oedipus complex, and later she had also begun to substitute a slightly older brother in place of her father. A comparison between her own and her brother's genitals had left a strong impression on her. Importantly, Freud emphasized that the girl had never been neurotic and had no hysterical symptoms. Nothing in her history seemed to lead to her homosexuality. Around the age of thirteen, she displayed a strong affection for a neighbor's young boy, perhaps reflecting the desire to be a mother. However, she quickly grew indifferent to him, and began taking an interest in mature, but still youthful women. A radical change occurred when she was sixteen, when her mother became pregnant and a third brother was born the following year. Before this event, Freud theorized, the girl's libido had taken a maternal attitude, whereas afterwards she developed homosexual tendencies. Thus, his paper on the case aimed to explain the riddle of the girl's homosexuality and to develop his discussion of sexuality.[28]

Freud's Explanations of Female Homosexuality

From 1905 to 1920

The 1920 case study of female homosexuality was an important text in the context of Freud's overall work on the topic of homosexuality and it is therefore important to place it alongside his other writings. Freud's basic stance in "Three Essays on the Theory of Sexuality" (1905) was that homosexuality was a fixation at an earlier stage of sexual development, which usually ended in heterosexuality. Therefore, all humans start from an innate bisexual disposition and maintain a residual homosexual desire, even if they eventually become heterosexuals. Although Freud saw homosexuals as individuals who remained fixated or inhibited, unlike many of his contemporaries, Freud insisted that they were not in any way ill.[29] Thus, in 1905, Freud undermined any simple notions of normality and pathology and presented an understanding of human sexuality that diverged further from other contemporary models. Freud's views changed over time, but he generally remained true to the 1905 position that all forms of adult sexuality are the product of a complex evolution that develops over time, from earliest infancy in the first relation with the mother.[30] In the "Three Essays," Freud used the word "inversion" for homosexuality rather than "perversion."[31] For Freud, homosexuality was an inversion because it was a deviation from the choice of a sexual object of the opposite sex; he probably also preferred the less pejorative term. Thus, he borrowed the medical idiom "inversion" from sexologists such as Krafft-Ebing and Ellis—who early on regarded it as a biological reversal between the sexes though they later developed more nuanced views—to talk instead of what was in essence a "mental inversion."[32] This was one example of Freud being influenced by, and building upon the work of, the sexologists while also becoming critical and breaking away from them in ways elaborated below.[33]

A broader framework is needed here to understand Freud's system of classification regarding the sexual instinct. Freud dedicated the first essay of the "Three Essays" to what he called "the sexual aberrations." He began by attacking the popular idea that the nature and characteristics of the sexual instinct were absent in childhood, appeared during puberty in connection with the process of coming to maturity, and were revealed in the attraction of one sex to the other with the presumed aim of sexual union. In contrast, he contended that such a simple description gave a false picture of human sexuality, and proposed instead to divide the discussion on the sexual instinct into deviations in respect of the *sexual object* and deviations of *the sexual aim.* [34]

It was under the subtitle "Deviations in Respect of the Sexual Object" in the first essay where Freud first discussed what he called "inversion." Under the same subtitle, he also included those who chose "sexually immature persons" (that is, children) as sexual objects and those who chose animals. However, under the subtitle "Deviations in Respect of the Sexual Aim," Freud included different deviations, which he concluded diverged from the "normal sexual aim" that he defined as "the union of the genitals in the act known as copulation, which leads to a release of the sexual tension and a temporary extinction of the sexual instinct—a satisfaction analogous to the sating of hunger."[35] He noted that even in the most normal sexual process we may detect rudiments which, if they developed, would lead to the deviations described as "perversions" (here choosing to employ this word). He defined perversions as "sexual activities which either (a) extend, in an anatomical sense, beyond the regions of the body that are designed for sexual union, or (b) linger over the intermediate relations to the sexual object which should normally be traversed rapidly on the path towards the final sexual aim."[36] Such perversions of the sexual aim could include, for example, "anatomical extensions" in the form of fetishism. Freud described some cases in which the normal sexual object is replaced by something which bears some relation to it, but is entirely unsuited to serve the normal sexual aim. These perversions could also be "fixations of preliminary sexual aims," which included fixation on looking in the form of scopophilia. Or they could include sadism and masochism, which for Freud were the most common and most significant of all perversions, namely the desire to inflict pain upon the sexual object and its reverse.[37]

However, it is "inversion," classified as a deviation in respect of the sexual object, that is of most interest to us here. Inversion was defined by him as those situations in which a man's sexual object is a man not a woman, and a woman's sexual object is a woman not a man. Freud speculated that the number of inverts was considerable and thereafter he made key points and arguments that he would return to in different ways in the years to come.

One of his central points in 1905 with regard to inverts was focused on their behavior. Freud insisted that inverts varied greatly in their behavior and there could be no generalization of their acts. They may be absolute inverts and thus their sexual objects were exclusively of their own sex; or they could be "amphigenic inverts, that is psycho-sexual hermaphrodites," thus lacking the characteristic of exclusiveness and choosing sexual objects of their own or the opposite sex. Alternatively, they could be "contingent inverts" who, under certain external conditions, were capable of taking someone of their own sex as their sexual object. Inverts could also vary widely in their own views regarding the peculiarity of their sexual instinct. "Some of them accept their inversion as something in the natural course of things, just as a normal person accepts the direction of his libido, and insist energetically that inversion is as legitimate as the normal attitude; others rebel against their inversion and feel it as a pathological compulsion." Other variations in the behavior of inverts might relate to questions of time: some might feel that the inversion existed from their very early childhood, while in others it "may constitute an episode on the way to a normal development."[38] Many authorities, Freud noted, would be unwilling to group all the different cases together and would prefer to lay stress upon their differences rather than their similarities, in accordance with their own preferred view of inversion. Nevertheless, though these distinctions cannot be disputed, it was impossible, Freud believed, to overlook the existence of numerous intermediate examples of every type. This led him to conclude that he was dealing with a connected series of the same phenomenon.

As early as 1905, Freud argued against any medical idea that inversion was an innate indication of nervous degeneracy or nervous diseases, fiercely rejecting the idea that it was innate or degenerate. Inverts, he argued, could not be regarded as degenerate as inversion was found, for example, in people who exhibited no other serious deviations from the normal. Moreover, it was also found in people whose efficiency was unimpaired, and who were "distinguished by specially high intellectual development and ethical culture."[39] It was also impossible to regard inversion as a sign of degeneracy as inversion was such a frequent and common phenomenon in history, up to the present day. To Freud, the diverse manifestations of inversion implied that it was also not innate, as sexologists like Havelock Ellis would have it, at least in regard to the exclusive types of inverts. Freud concluded that he was "forced to a suspicion that the choice between 'innate' and 'acquired' is not an exclusive one or that it does not cover all the issues involved in inversion."[40] In 1905, Freud also rejected the theory of hermaphroditism that presupposed that an inverted man was like a woman, being susceptible to the charms of masculine attributes, both physical and mental, and feeling like a woman in search of a man. Instead, he argued that while this seemed true in some cases, a large proportion of male inverts, in fact, retained the mental quality of masculinity, and possessed relatively few of the secondary characteristics of the opposite sex; what they sought in their sexual objects were feminine mental traits. Additionally, Freud emphasized that inverts did not have one single sexual aim; what united them was only an inversion vis-à-vis sexual object.[41]

We should remember the broader context: in the late nineteenth-century medical literature, the term "sexual inversion" did not carry the same meaning as "homosexuality," but referred to a broad range of deviant sexual behavior rather than to the sex of the love-object.[42] Early on it signified a total reversal of one's sexual role. In Ellis's early writings, for example, a woman could not invert any aspect of her gender role without inverting the whole. Thus, for Victorians, a complete reversal of a woman's sexual character to masculinity was required for her to act as a female homosexual.[43] However, by 1900, there was a clear shift as medicine began narrowing and classifying sexual deviations into more discrete categories. Thus, the historian George Chauncey argued that Freud's 1905 text with its introduction of the distinction between aim and object was "a highly significant change at a particular moment in the intellectual history of sexuality." Thereafter, researchers increasingly distinguished passive or active sexual behavior from sexual objects, which became the more important element of classification, eventually leading to "homosexual" replacing "invert," though more so regarding male rather than female homosexuality.[44] Furthermore, after 1900, the medical profession also predominantly (though at times with reservations) accepted the congenital theory in the explanation not only of inversion but of other supposed mental illnesses. In 1905, however, Freud's starting point was a direct challenge to the hegemony of the congenital theory.[45]

The subject of homosexuality appeared frequently in Freud's writing in relation to different clinical innovative formulations and discussions. Flanders et al. note the different themes in his work on this topic.[46] They state that in his discussion of feminism and feminine sexuality,

> Freud is not immune from betraying a vernacular prejudice in his writing, although, in relation to homosexuality, he is often at pains to identify it, illuminate it, and distance himself from it. In principle, he takes a distanced and nonjudgmental position, however much he is aware of the fact that the subject is coloured always by social attitudes, the cultural life which is always informing the researcher and his subject.[47]

Beyond his basic stand that remained developmental, as expressed in 1905, Flanders et al. note that a significant relevant consistency in Freud's thinking about homosexuality was indeed his belief—which he never thoroughly explained but took as axiomatic, or as a fundamental paradigm—that every individual's starting point was an innate bisexuality, which was both biological and psychological.[48] Furthermore, Freud believed that bisexuality was always present in cases of homosexuality and, therefore, there was an element of heterosexuality in the homosexual object choice, something he emphasized in 1920 in particular. In fact, for Freud, bisexuality was the normal baseline and a universal starting point of all sexuality, and he stressed this in the 1920 case.[49] Earlier, in 1909, Freud emphasized: "There is absolutely no justification for distinguishing a special homosexual instinct. What constitutes a homosexual is a peculiarity not in his instinctual life but in his choice of an object." In a footnote that he added in 1915 to the "Three Essays," he clarified that:

> Psycho-analytic research is most decidedly opposed to any attempt at separating off homosexuals from the rest of mankind as a group of a special character. By studying sexual excitations other than those that are manifestly displayed, it has found that all human beings are capable of making a homosexual object-choice and have in fact made one in their unconscious.[50]

Another element in Freud's thinking about homosexuality, the nature of object choice and the possible path to a homosexual object choice, was developed in relation to his theory of narcissism. In a footnote added to the "Three Essays" in 1910, he wrote:

> Future inverts, in the earliest years of their childhood, pass through a phase of very intense but short-lived fixation to a woman (usually their mother) and after leaving this behind, they identify themselves with a woman and take themselves as their sexual object. That is to say, they proceed from a narcissistic basis, and look for a young man who resembles themselves and whom they may love as their mother loved them.[51]

In 1914, Freud elaborated this idea further, stating that the powerful immersion in the first relationship with the mother is a potential basis for the development of a homosexual object choice. This was because an overwhelming attachment would then be maintained and ameliorated by taking a love-object based on the self, while the subject identified with the caring but overwhelming mother.[52] Freud also linked the specific narcissistic anxiety associated with sexual object choice with fears of castration; hence homosexual object choice is one solution to the castration anxiety of the male.[53] But for Freud, the effects of castration were also significant in female development. In his 1920 discussion of the homosexual object choice of Margarethe Csonka, Freud added the narcissistic threat of bodily "disfigurement" due to maternity associated with childbearing as another condition potentially driving homosexual object choice.[54]

Flanders et al. identify another theme in Freud's various references to homosexuality, namely that "Freud does not offer unequivocal support for any firm position in a debate about the normality or pathology of homosexuality, although he acknowledges intermittently the cultural context in which this debate, like his research, is situated."[55] His overall commitment was to deepen understanding about what others called normality and pathology, rather than to take a position in a debate to which he nonetheless referred. He often related to the social forces which influenced the individual's sexual development, and which also impinged on any study of sexuality. Early on, Freud was careful to use quotation marks when addressing homosexuality and referred in 1916–1917, for example, to "perverse" people to distance himself from this word. As noted, in the first essay in the "Three Essays," Freud described homosexuality as an "inversion" not a perversion to emphasize how much it was tied to the choice of object and not to anything specific in the drive or aim. In this sense, homosexuality was an aid to his conceptualization of instincts, loosening any conventional assumption regarding the direct link of instinct or object. Though to Freud homosexuality signified a failure to move towards adult heterosexuality and heterosexual intercourse, and though homosexuality did not subordinate the sexual drive to the reproductive function (which appears only in adolescence), Freud insisted that homosexual object choice was normal in origin and that homosexuality was part of every infantile experience: we have all been homosexual in infancy and childhood and homosexuality lives on in the unconscious life of the adult. He continuously reminded his readers, as he did in 1920, that "In all of us, throughout life, the libido normally oscillates between male and female objects, the bachelor gives up his men friends when he marries and returns to club life when married life has lost its savour."[56]

By 1935, Freud even famously wrote in a letter to a mother concerned about the homosexuality of her son:

> Homosexuality is assuredly no advantage, but it is nothing to be ashamed of, no vice, no degradation, it cannot be classified as an illness; we [psychoanalysts] consider it to be a variation of the sexual function produced by certain arrest of sexual development. Many highly respectable individuals of ancient and modern times have been homosexuals ... It is a great injustice to persecute homosexuality as a crime—and a cruelty, too.[57]

Thus, while Freud did view homosexuals as different, he did not see them as ill or as sinners or criminals, and he described them in increasingly nonjudgmental and neutral terms.[58]

The 1920 text should be seen as part of this change, providing a missing link between the 1905 hypothesis and 1935 perspective while maintaining Freud's 1905 view that sexual object choice is more important than character inversion.[59] As we shall see below, he also continued his criticism of the continual biological-congenital emphasis of some sexologists (though their ideas became more complex). In 1920, Freud rejected the theory of common hermaphroditism, such as that of the Hanoverian lawyer, jurist, and journalist Karl Heinrich Ulrichs (1825–1895) who saw male inversion as representing "a woman's spirit in a man's body." He also rejected the theories of the English utopian socialist, poet, and philosopher Edward Carpenter (1844–1929) and the German physician, sexologist, and early advocate for sexual minorities Magnus Hirschfeld (1868–1935) who raised the option of an "intermediate sex."[60] Overall, it was Freud's 1920 discussion of the first full case of a self-declared same-sex love and female homosexuality that further contributed to his radicalism towards male homosexuality as well. The 1920 paper is undoubtedly phallocentric, and equates everyday and sexual activity in women with masculinity; but in contrast to those who emphasize the conservative elements of the text and the fact that heterosexuality for Freud was the ideal norm for mature sexuality,[61] I believe that, overall, it should be seen as radical for the immediate postwar period. This, together with his meetings with the young woman, led Freud to openly admit that his patient was completely healthy, neither neurotic nor hysterical; he warded off any expectations of a "cure" and took a broader stance towards society's and her parents' homophobia.[62]

The 1920 text was part of a shift whereby female patients came to dominate psychoanalytic debates about homosexuality, and interest turned from male to female homosexuality in texts by Ernest Jones, Joan Riviere, and Helene Deutsch, among others.[63] In the final case of 1920, Freud revisited the case study model having already begun to move beyond this genre of thinking and writing. Here he developed his 1905 stand on universal bisexuality and multivalent sexuality more clearly, while critically challenging his patient's story and contextualizing her family circumstances.[64]

Mother Substitution and Oedipal Drama

So, what were Freud's particular views of female homosexuality in 1920? Setting biology aside and adopting a psychological view, Freud's first explanation for the girl's homosexual choice was that the beloved lady was a substitute for her mother. However, he went further, tying homo- and heterosexuality together rather than seeing them as opposing poles. He proposed that the lady's slender figure, beauty, and forthright manner reminded the girl of an older brother: "Her latest choice corresponded, therefore, not only to her feminine but also to her masculine ideal; it combined satisfaction of the homosexual tendency with that of the heterosexual one."[65]

Freud noted that the girl had little cause to feel affection for her mother. Still youthful herself, the mother saw in her daughter a sexual competitor. She favored the sons, limited the girl's independence, and restricted any closeness between the girl and her father. A yearning for a kinder mother seemed to make sense. Freud insisted, however, on yet another explanation for the turn to homosexuality, suggesting that the shift in the girl was really triggered by the mental process attached to

the birth of her new brother. Why was this so momentous in influencing the girl's sexual proclivity? Freud's complex answer was that just
when the girl was experiencing the revival of her infantile Oedipus
complex at puberty, the birth of the brother made her suffer a psychological disappointment. At the time, the girl became conscious of
her wish to have a male child, though she was not conscious of desiring her father's child. With the birth of the brother, it was her uncon-
sciously hated rival who gave birth to a male child from her father.
Thus, resentful and embittered, the girl turned away from her father
and from men altogether. This had a lasting effect as, "After this first
great reverse she forswore her womanhood and sought another goal
for her libido."[66] Freud then explained that "this girl had entirely
repudiated her wish for a child, her love of men, and the feminine role
in general."[67]

In subtle ways, female homosexuality was interpreted by Freud as part
of the Oedipal family drama and as connected to heterosexuality. The
girl's repudiation of the wish for a child led Freud to push his logic further and claim that this female homosexual had, in effect, "changed into
a man." Apparently, he meant by this that (1) she took her mother in
place of her father as the object of her love; and (2) she behaved like a
chivalrous male lover towards her beloved lady. Indeed, seeing desire and
activity solely in masculine terms is theoretically the phallocentric, limiting logic of the paper. Nonetheless, we should not miss the point that this
paradoxical text includes historically radical aspects that move beyond
this logic, accepting the girl's love not as an illness, but rather as real in
its intensity for a variety of psychological reasons.

As noted, Freud put forward the idea that female homosexuality
was also a search for a better mother. He wrote that it was easy for the
girl "to revive her earlier love for her mother and with its help to bring
about an overcompensation for her current hostility towards her."[68]
Yet again, he complicated this idea further by placing homosexuality
within a heterosexual matrix. By turning to homosexuality, there was
a secondary gain derived from the girl's actual relations with her
mother.[69] By becoming homosexual, the girl left men to her mother
thereby removing what was partly responsible for her mother's dislike
of her. Furthermore, the girl's new homosexual position was reinforced by the fact that it displeased her father: she could take revenge
on him for disciplining her for loving women. Henceforth, Freud
concluded, the girl remained homosexual also out of defiance against
her father.[70] The girl's psychological "inversion" received its final
reinforcement when she found in her lady an object that satisfied both
her homo- and heterosexual libidinal tendencies.

Female Homosexuality and Early Twentieth-Century Heterosexual Masculinity

Although many factors led to the young woman's turn to homosexuality, Freud repeatedly connected it to heterosexual masculinity. He described her behavior towards her lady as characteristic of masculine romantic love in the early twentieth century. (Indeed, as I will show in Part II, it seems that it was this rather than any medical model on which she relied for her same-sex love.)[71] For example, the girl hoped for just a little attention while asking for nothing in return; she made pilgrimages to places visited by her beloved; and she kept silent about any other sensual desires. She acted, in short, like a Christian gentleman of the Viennese upper class.[72] Although she was "a well-brought-up and modest girl," she was not in the least repelled by her beloved's bad reputation. She courted women who were heterosexual "coquettes in the ordinary sense of the word," while rejecting the advances made by a homosexual friend of her own age. Her lady's bad reputation was a "necessary condition for love."[73] For Freud, these seemingly illogical actions were logical in light of the masculine type of object choice derived from the mother: it was a necessary condition that the loved object should be of bad repute sexually. When the girl later learned the extent to which her adored lady made a living as a prostitute, her reaction—again somewhat typical of a Christian gentleman of the time—was compassionate and involved plans for rescuing her beloved.[74] Thus, vis-à-vis her lady, the girl took on the masculine role of heterosexual courtship befitting the time. Freud summarized:

> She displayed the humility and the sublime overvaluation of the sexual object so characteristic of the male lover, the renunciation of all narcissistic satisfaction, and the preference for being the lover rather than the beloved. She had thus not only chosen a feminine love-object but had also developed a masculine attitude towards that object.[75]

Freud also argued that from her early childhood the girl had a strongly marked "masculinity complex." He wrote:

> A spirited girl, always ready for romping and fighting, she was not at all prepared to be second to her slightly older brother; after inspecting his genital organs, she had developed a pronounced envy for the penis, and the thoughts derived from this envy still

continued to fill her mind. She was in fact a feminist; she felt it to be unjust that girls should not enjoy the same freedom as boys, and rebelled against the lot of woman in general. At the time of the analysis the idea of pregnancy and child-birth was disagreeable to her, partly, I surmise, on account of the bodily disfigurement connected with them.[76]

The phrase "masculinity complex" was first used by the Dutch analyst J. H. Van Ophuijsen in 1917.[77] But beyond this theoretical reference, here Freud was connecting feminism with masculinity, a connection which was common among other fin-de-siècle medical men who wrote against first- and second-generation women in higher education. These doctors tried to stigmatize women's wish for rights and growing independence as abnormally masculine. It is important to note that, in contrast to them, Freud used the phrase "masculinity complex" much more neutrally; his theory was phallocentric but *not* derogatory towards the young woman's homosexuality or her feminism or her independent desire and passion. In this, too, Freud was more radical than some of the medical men of his time.

Freud and the Sexologists: The Cause and Nature of Homosexuality

In order to further contextualize Freud beyond his own writings over time, it makes sense to explore the medical and sexological circumstances in which he developed his ideas, and to delve more deeply into the detailed history of both the evolving term "sexual inversion" and the emerging field of sexology. Freud's views of homosexuality as a developmental inhibition stemming from universal bisexuality and his primarily psychological approach diverged further from some of the ideas commonly attributed to leading sexologists such as Krafft-Ebing, Moll, and Ellis. It is important, however, to situate Freud's views within these broader sexological debates in more exact ways in order to evaluate the kind of framework he was providing for his young female homosexual patient, and to accurately assess the radicalness or uniqueness of his views.

In his own writings on sexuality, Freud insisted that his opinions contrasted with those of the sexologists, who emphasized hereditary models, and from their predominantly congenital model that saw perversions as stemming from a hereditary and constitutional predisposition, or a later-acquired degeneration.[78] This was also the view of standard histories of psychoanalysis which saw Freud as standing in

contrast to the work of the sexologists.[79] In 1920, Freud even set his
ideas in sharp opposition to those of other sexologists to emphasize
both the exceptionalism and contrarian radicalism of his views.[80]
The early sexologists, however, were more complex than was evident
from Freud's presentation of them, and indeed more so than some
scholars assume. As new and revisionist scholarship shows, the sexologists' attitudes to homosexuality, in fact, also shifted and changed
over time, and their complexity persisted in contradictory views that
both pathologized perversion and articulated these changing attitudes.[81] However, this revisionist scholarship tends by implication to
downplay Freud's innovation and emphasize how much those who
preceded him foreshadowed many of his ideas.[82] A more balanced
view is needed here, I believe, to integrate the revisionist findings
about the sexologists without disregarding Freud's distinct contribution to the debate on homosexuality.[83] Situating Freud's ideas in the
context of the prevailing medical discourse reveals that Freud may
have been less unique in all aspects of his views on sexuality for his
time. Nonetheless, I will show how he was still both more innovative
and radical than has been assumed, and more so than the later feminist readings judged him to be as they took him out of context, particularly when he took the sexologists' ideas a step further in
discussing the 1920 case of female homosexuality.

"Sexual Inversion" in Men and Women

I have given above some of the broader context for understanding the
term "sexual inversion" in the nineteenth century, but it is worth
exploring the origins of this concept. In fact, the term "inversion" in
reference to same-sex and/or gender inversion emerged in very particular historical circumstances during debates concerning the process
leading up to the legal foundation of a unified German Empire in 1871.
From thereon it rapidly became central to same-sex studies in other
countries by the end of the century, most notably perhaps in Havelock
Ellis's 1897 publication *Sexual Inversion*.[84] Karl Heinrich Ulrichs
introduced the term "uranism" in 1864 and the idea of "sexual inversion" to discuss in positive terms the love of men for other men; and,
in an 1870 pamphlet, he used it in his Latin formulation of the invert
as someone with "a female soul confined in a male body." He also
noted briefly that a woman who loves women would be "a male
soul ... confined to the female body," but what motivated his discussion was his wish to oppose the possible criminalization of men who
loved men in all German states. In the 1860s, Prussia increasingly

dominated the political landscape, and thereby threatened to replace the different legal statutes of the sovereign German states with its own penal code. Most of the other states had already gradually eliminated the medieval prohibitions on male and female sodomy that had been on their law books. Many of the penal codes of small states such as Ulrichs's native Hanover followed the more moderate Napoleonic Code and did not criminalize same-sex acts. In contrast, Prussia still criminalized same-sex behavior under Paragraph 143 of its penal code. Due to Prussia's rising power, Ulrichs was highly concerned that Prussia's penal law would most likely be imposed across other states. He therefore began campaigning: he started a lobby against the criminalization of men who loved men, and submitted for discussion a petition demanding that "the inborn love for men" be decriminalized in all German states. His petition was rejected and what he had worried about became a reality. In 1871, Prussia's anti-male, same-sex legislation was adopted across the unified German Empire as Paragraph 175 in the penal code. The new law linked sexual behavior to citizenship by punishing male same-sex practices with possible revocation of civil rights. Female same-sex acts were not criminalized by the Prussian or German imperial penal codes, reflecting the fact that women were excluded from full citizenship.[85] Activism on behalf of homosexual rights developed in the German-speaking world and increased with the passing of Germany's Paragraph 175 and Paragraph 129b of Austria's 1852 criminal code criminalizing both female and male homosexuality.[86]

Thus, prior to psychoanalysis, medical ideas on sexuality developed in close association with legal debates, forensic medicine, and the analysis of criminals as moral offenders. Around the 1870s, psychiatrists began to look at perceived acts of immorality as signs of an innate morbid condition, arguing that irregular sexual behavior should not be regarded as a sin or a crime but as the symptom of pathology, and that rather than being punished as criminals sex offenders should be treated as patients. German and French psychiatrists such as Carl von Westphal, Richard von Krafft-Ebing, Jean-Martin Charcot, and Paul Moreau de Tours shifted the focus away from discussions about immorality to arguments concerning evolutionary thinking or deterministic theories of hereditary degeneration and neuropsychological automatism. They started explaining perversions as inborn deviance (a concept that in public debates could be read in both negative and positive ways, as for and against homosexuality).[87] In the mid-1880s, Krafft-Ebing, the most prominent psychiatrist of his time in central Europe and a founding father of the scientific field of sexology, initiated a move away from psychiatric thinking in which deviant sexuality was seen as episodic and symptomatic of a more fundamental mental disorder, and towards considering perversion as an integral part of sexuality more generally. This was further elaborated by Albert Moll in the 1890s.[88]

The early medical debates on inversion and the reactions to them were male-dominated. The leading sexologists focused their writings on male homosexuality and most of the case studies they wrote focused on male subjects,[89] especially as in most European countries it was only male homosexuality that was prohibited by law. In the late nineteenth century, therefore, discussion of female inversion was more limited.[90]

There were other differences in the discussions of male and female inversion beyond the legal framework. As explained above, the discourse of male inversion was tied both to debates surrounding the rising modern state and to sexual identity and male same-sex practices. In contrast, female inversion was mostly connected to issues of social rather than sexual difference, at least initially, and to the changing roles of men and women. For that reason, the notion of female inversion was also attached to the broader cultural discourse concerning the "woman question" and women's rights at the turn of the century and the subsequent early decades. Such discussions included misogynist responses to feminism, often focusing on the perceived "manliness" of the New Woman or her transgressive divergence in appearance, behavior, and actions from traditional gender roles.[91]

Krafft-Ebing's early engagement with female same-sex sexuality in his key publication *Psychopathia Sexualis* illustrates more broadly the increasingly complex meanings of female inversion at the turn of the century. Heike Bauer argues that when Krafft-Ebing's book first came out in 1886, and when he briefly discussed female inversion, two issues were at stake.[92] The first was the establishment of the existence of female sexuality beyond reproduction. He argued against the idea that women are not capable of committing sexual acts with other women and insisted that, like men, women who have sex with other women are physiologically able to produce "orgasm, including ejaculation by means of a sexual act, and hence sexual satisfaction."[93] The second issue that mattered to him was recognition of same-sex practices between women, but his argument was convoluted and aimed primarily at decriminalizing sex between men. If female same-sex sexuality was ignored by German legislation, then criminalizing males was surely naïve and incoherent and therefore erroneous, he stressed. Krafft Ebing developed the argument that sexual inversion in men and women was a natural phenomenon, and that it would be appropriate to decriminalize male homosexuality rather than criminalize females as well.[94]

Although female inversion was marginal in Krafft-Ebing's writings in the original German, he did specifically address the under-representation of women in sexological studies and the insufficient empirical material available on the topic. He predicted that this knowledge would expand with the entry of women into this field of medicine. However, his politics were not part of the progressive same-sex or feminist activism of the later nineteenth century.[95] In 1889, for example, he included female homosexuality in his discussion of perversions and divided lesbianism into four categories specifying degrees of homosexual deviance, each fusing sexual, physiological, and social characteristics. The degrees escalated from women with no external masculine characteristics to those who showed degenerative and pathological homosexuality in their bodies, behavior, and appearance.[96]

In his first category he included women who "did not betray their anomaly by external appearance or by mental (masculine) sexual characteristics," though when physically examined they could display a masculine formation of the larynx. These women were responsive to the approaches of more masculine women. In his second category were women with a "strong preference for male garments"; in the third, when inversion was fully developed, he stated that "the woman so acting assumes a definitely masculine role," and in the fourth category, which he called "gynandry," was "the extreme grade of degenerative homosexuality"—women who were feminine only by virtue of their genital organs but otherwise, in thought, sentiment, action, or appearance were masculine.[97]

Krafft-Ebing's medical views on female homosexuality were tied to ideas about the shift in social gender roles of the time. As historian Smith-Rosenberg observed,

> Krafft-Ebing did not focus on the sexual behavior of the women he categorized as lesbian but, rather, on their social behavior and physical appearance. In every case study, Krafft-Ebing linked lesbianism to the rejection of conventional female roles, to cross-dressing, and to 'masculine' physiological traits.[98]

Reporting on one female homosexual patient, for example, he believed that she was quite conscious of her "pathological condition," even adding that she had a "deep voice, manly gait, without beard, small breasts; cropped her hair short and gave the impression of a man in women's clothes."[99] Indeed, in her influential reading, Smith-Rosenberg claims that, from the 1890s, male physicians like him began attacking the respectability of the New Woman, and shifted the definition of female deviance from the New Woman's rejection of motherhood to their perceived rejection of men. Educated and autonomous women who lived outside of heterosexual marriage emerged as "unnaturally" sexual.[100]

To understand how Krafft-Ebing reached these ambivalent views, I will examine the development of his and others' ideas to show how sexology was in essence a dynamic and contradictory field in general. This will help to clarify where we should situate Freud in this debate that was more dynamic than he presented yet to which he made an important contribution.

Sexology in Flux

As mentioned above, new revisionist scholarship further emphasized the extent to which the early sexologists altered their views over time, and how they can therefore be seen as conflicted actors—both pathologizing homosexuality and allowing for progressive ways of thinking about it before Freud. Perhaps the key example was Krafft-Ebing himself, who shifted from his moral judgment of perversion and homosexuality to a more lenient and humanitarian attitude. From the early 1890s, he actively opposed the criminalization of homosexual acts. Examining the different editions of his magnus opus *Psychopathia Sexualis* (there were at least thirty-five British and American editions between 1892 and 1899), historian Harry Oosterhuis effectively demonstrates that Krafft-Ebing became more sympathetic towards homosexuality, especially as more middle- and upper-class male patients and correspondents shared their life stories with him.[101] Gradually, Krafft-Ebing presented himself as impartial and against traditional moral-religious and legal denunciations of sexual deviance as sin or crime. Middle- and upper-class men (women did not write to Krafft-Ebing) labelled homosexuals had the choice to read and react to medical work in different ways, and they influenced a shift in his views. Their life stories, therefore, played a role in the production of knowledge on sexuality, and helped to change his views as he added more patients' and correspondents' accounts from one edition of his book to the next.[102]

When Krafft-Ebing was in the early stages of his career, he was influenced by the natural-scientific approach in psychiatry that aimed to classify mental diseases on the basis of anatomical pathology. At the same time, Krafft-Ebing's work collected and presented a growing number of case histories. Thus, he started to focus more on individuals' biographies than on the specific characteristics of a particular illness.[103] After the first edition of *Psychopathia Sexualis* appeared in German in 1886, it was followed by seventeen expanded editions in German alone between 1886 and 1924, and by translations in several languages, thereby becoming the standard in the field. Krafft-Ebing revised the book several times and added new categories and case histories over time.[104]

Beyond the broad political context regarding male citizenship, Krafft-Ebing's interest in perversions emerged out of his experience in asylum psychiatry and his preoccupation with forensic medicine for criminal acts like sodomy. *Psychopathia Sexualis* was initially aimed at lawyers and doctors discussing sexual crimes in court. His basic stand, common among liberal physicians in 1870 to 1900, was that in many cases perversion was a disease. Thus, deviant—that is, non-reproductive—sexual acts were regarded as symptoms of an illness caused by natural phenomena, and therefore he believed that most sex offenders should be treated as patients suffering from mental diseases, unable to control their sexual drives, rather than be punished. Krafft-Ebing's distinction between immoral "perversity" and ailing "perversion" shifted the focus away from immoral and criminal acts that were temporary to a discussion of pathological conditions. In this he was influenced by nineteenth-century neuropathology and theories of degeneration that explained mental illness and sexual disorders. He was inspired by the evolutionary theories of Charles Darwin, and even more by those of the French alienist Bénédict Augustin Morel. After Morel, who focused on heredity as the underlying cause of mental illness, Krafft-Ebing argued that the strains of modern civilization on the nervous system caused mental disturbances that could also be inherited from one generation to the next. Krafft-Ebing believed that perversion might be acquired through the bad influence of others, but he increasingly emphasized that many sexual disorders were inborn; in an 1877 publication on sexual pathology, he assumed that degeneration was the underlying cause of inborn perversion.[105]

A close reading of *Psychopathia Sexualis* from around 1890 onwards shows that though the book was characterized by some scholars as the climax of the medicalization of sexuality and Victorian hypocrisy, this work, as Oosterhuis argued, was contradictory in nature and cannot be regarded as merely disqualifying sexual aberrations. Krafft-Ebing's changing views were not coherent and his scientific approach to sexuality was ambivalent. On the one hand, Krafft-Ebing had a clear wish to differentiate between health (tied to reproduction) and pathology. But, on the other hand, he admitted a graded scale of health and illness rather than a clear binary. Normal sexuality could also include features of perverse desire. For example, sadism was a pathological extension of the normal sexual psychology of males for Krafft-Ebing. In addition, he blurred the boundary between masculinity and femininity in his discussion of inversion, even hinting that absolute masculinity and femininity might be mere abstractions. This led Oosterhuis to argue that although Krafft-Ebing's biological approach to sexuality has often been contrasted with Freud's, which was psychological (most famously stated by Peter Gay in his standard biography of Freud), in *Psychopathia Sexualis* there is an inconsistency between organic explanations and clinical descriptions.[106] Oosterhuis adds that although in his case histories Krafft-Ebing often mentioned physical examinations of his patients' sexual organs, or if they had died anatomies of their brains, these were less relevant to his definitions of perversions. Oosterhuis sees Krafft-Ebing as taking a step away from forensic focus and physiological explanations towards a psychological approach to human sexuality. Although the underlying causes of perversions remained degeneration and heredity for Krafft-Ebing, he moved the medical discussion in a more psychological direction. For this reason and because he viewed human sexuality as distinct from animal instincts, for Oosterhuis, he foreshadowed Freud.[107]

His statements about the expected degeneration in "perverts" notwithstanding, Krafft-Ebing's gradual shift towards treating wealthier, better-educated clients (rather than lower-class patients in custodial care) meant that he attended to those who could speak up for themselves and even criticize his labeling of them as pathological. These almost exclusively male cases, collected in the 1880s, could tell him that they neither felt unhealthy nor unnatural. This must have influenced Krafft-Ebing who published their affirming accounts of themselves as suffering from legal and social obstacles rather than from any pathology, without adding any medical comment. In subsequent editions, he included more such cases of uranists who declared that they sought no cure. Initially, Krafft-Ebing did not attack the German and Austrian laws against "unnatural vice." But, in the 1890s, he was among the first to sign Magnus Hirschfeld's petition advocating the abolition of Paragraph 175, and he supported the homosexual rights movement funded in Berlin in 1897 by Hirschfeld. In the early 1900s, Krafft-Ebing admitted that his earlier views had been too one sided.

He was, therefore, influenced by his patients who sought under-standing, acceptance, and support from him and, as Oosterhuis argues, in the context of his time he showed a degree of open-mind-edness and pragmatism.[108] Krafft-Ebing continued to experiment with hypnosis to cure perversion, but applied it only at his patients' request. Curing perversion was marginal to his work and he made it clear that in cases of inborn perversion a cure was unlikely.[109]

Though I emphasize that the early sexologists did not have the same scope as Freud in ways I will explain below, both Krafft-Ebing and his follower Moll can still be seen as heralding a new modern under-standing of human sexuality before Freud. They anticipated, for example, the Freudian assumption that sexual restraint may be an unhealthy repression, and that unfulfilled desire may lead to mental distress. Moll even acknowledged that sex was not harmful for homosexuals but could even be healthy.[110] Moreover, both Krafft-Ebing and Moll, like Freud later on, were pessimistic about what they saw as an irresolvable contradiction between the rational and moral order and, at times, violent sexual urges.[111]

The sexologists developed slightly different ideas on diverse topics, depending on the period. In relation to contrary sexual feelings, Krafft-Ebing, for example, had initially tended to closely identify inversion with degeneration. But in the mid-1890s, he and Moll were more influenced by embryological research and evolutionary thinking suggesting that early life is characterized by sexual indifference. In Moll's thinking, perversions were frequently accompanied by heredi-tary taints and nervous or hysterical disturbances—which could also stem from psychosocial circumstances—but he did not qualify them as mental disorders. Instead, he saw perversions as morbid-like (krankhafte) modifications of the normal sexual drive.[112]

Initially, Krafft-Ebing saw reproduction as distinguishing between normal sexuality and pathological perversion, but from the mid-1890s he shifted away from procreation as the main factor and focused on the dichotomy of heterosexuality and homosexuality as the basic sexual categories, and paid more attention to whether there was a relational and affective dimension of sexuality.[113] Oosterhuis sees Krafft-Ebing's model of sexuality as centering on desire instead of reproduction in a manner which is modern. He also sees Krafft-Ebing as marking a transition in the urban bourgeois milieu away from the Christian ethos in which reproduction dictates self-discipline and control of the passions towards a consumerist culture of abundance which valued the satisfaction of individual desire, perhaps especially in the cities.[114]

In his book on children, Moll also questioned the relationship between nature and nurture, and the causal role of congenital degeneration; he also examined whether perversion was acquired by psychological association or seduction.[115] With time, both Krafft-Ebing and Moll moved from a predominantly forensic and physiological focus on perversion to thinking about psychological issues beyond reproduction and towards the satisfaction of desire and even partnership.[116]

Thus, before Freud, psychiatrists had begun to shift from a biomedical perspective stressing physical features to one that also considered psychological aspects of sexual desire.[117] Though Krafft-Ebing and Moll were supporters of the degeneration theory and evolutionary explanations of sexuality at different times, Oosterhuis argues that they cannot simply be labeled as supporters of biological explanations (as Freud mostly called them). This is especially because although in their writing they both located the sexual drive in the nervous system and the brain, and understood the underlying causes of perversion as hereditary, in their practice they were simultaneously corresponding with homosexuals who challenged them, pushing the degeneration theory to the background and bringing psychology to the fore to a greater extent than had been recognized before this claim was made by the revisionist historiography. The case histories recounted by their patients and presented by the sexologists concentrated increasingly on personal history, inner feelings, and emotions; physiology and behavior counted less than the psychology that underpinned them. Sexuality became manifest in both internal and external phenomena whereby the physical affected the mind and the psychological affected the body in a complex interplay.[118] Thus, in ways that historians often disregarded, the sexologists began to shift from a biomedical perspective that emphasized physical features to one that also considered the psychological aspects of sexual desire.[119] This revisionist scholarship by Oosterhuis and others is important as it helps us to understand anew the nuances surrounding the work of the leading sexologists, the complexities of sexology, and its important contributions. But to me it is also important in that it reveals the distinct differences that clearly remained between the sexologists and Freud who started from a more radical position. Freud developed each of the key sexologists' ideas further in ways I will indicate and elucidate below, and in the 1920s he did so in significant ways.

Krafft-Ebing and Freud

We can indeed detect similarities between Freud and Krafft-Ebing who, as I have demonstrated, should not be seen merely as standing at opposite poles. Whereas the famous sexologist and homosexual rights activist Magnus Hirschfeld focused on studying the "third sex," Krafft-Ebing (especially in his later formulations) and Freud were interested in sexuality in more general terms. Neither saw homosexuality as a crime or moral failure, and they supported its decriminalization.[120]

However, the differences between Krafft-Ebing and Freud were clear and therefore Freud was not wrong to emphasize the difference between his own views and those of Krafft-Ebing. The subtle shifts in Krafft-Ebing's views, let us not forget, were only clarified after much later historical research into his dialogue and correspondence with his patients. Moreover, Krafft-Ebing still fluctuated in a contradictory manner between stigmatizing sexual variation as mental illness and recognizing the possibility of unique individual desires. As Oosterhuis writes, his work on sexual pathology was indeed a reflection of the anxieties of fin-de-siècle bourgeois culture.[121] It was Freud, I stress, who moved towards a twentieth-century view of these ideas, and he began where Krafft-Ebing ended.

Krafft-Ebing shifted towards normalizing perversion by giving "perverts" a voice and by beginning to blur the distinction between normality and abnormality. By contrast, Freud's embrace of the normal was tied to radically destabilizing its meaning. As Birgit Lang argues, Freud's dialogic-psychoanalytic case study can be seen as an inversion of the very genre.[122] Whereas Krafft-Ebing relied on an academic framing and style of writing, Freud used particularization and limited the case to a specific aspect in order to mediate the tension between individual case history and generalization. Thus, Freud made the case study the site of theory formation on a much grander scale, pushing and blurring terms such as "normal" and "abnormal" further than Krafft-Ebing, and acknowledging non-reproductive desires with less of the physical, hereditary, and degeneration baggage that Kraft-Ebbing carried.[123]

Freud drew on Krafft-Ebing's concepts and terminology, yet, as Lang argues too, rather than charting and recording perversions, Freud's theory of sexuality made homosexuality more acceptable and stripped it of its pathological undertones. Both Krafft-Ebing and the early Freud can be identified as progressive for their time as both understood homosexuals to have the capacity to live productive lives, and both supported the idea that homosexuality was not a crime. But Krafft-Ebing engaged with what is and should be normal mostly implicitly by giving his patients and correspondents a mediated stage on which to present their own views of their social predicaments. For

Freud, the normal was something to directly question and challenge much more thoroughly as part of the process of formulating his theories.[124] Thus, Freud expanded Krafft-Ebing's work by destabilizing the boundaries between normal and homosexuality and presenting a grand theory of sexuality with broader implications.

Freud tied homosexuality to normality and normality to homosexuality in a Gordian knot. He also conceptualized the fear of homosexuality as crucial in the formation of neurosis and psychosis. Lang adds: "His interest in internal psychological processes also meant that new facets of homosexual life started to become imaginable—including abnormal psychical states."[125] Freud gave us a new complexity in understanding homosexuality as part of sexuality generally that was entirely lacking in the discussions of other sexologists.[126]

Freud can be seen as building on such interventions in the early conceptualization of modern Western sexuality that tied it to endless self-scrutiny, the fear of being abnormal, and the formation of sexual identities. In the 1920 case of female homosexuality, his ideas on sexual variation were perhaps less exceptional among his peers than his presentation of them assumed, but he was nevertheless a developer who advanced the discussion the furthest.[127]

It is interesting to note the place of female patients in the early sexological writings vis-à-vis the more central role (sometimes more active and other times more passive) that they played in psychoanalysis. Unlike Krafft-Ebing's male patients and correspondents who wrote to him of their own volition, the majority of his female patients did not engage with him voluntarily; they may have been transferred to his care by a husband or caretaker or through involvement in various kinds of court proceedings. Accordingly, the encounters between Krafft-Ebing and his female patients were imbued with tension and resistance absent in the exchange with his male correspondents.[128] He wrote of one hospitalized female patient that she "could only be restrained from lewd attacks on other female patients through diligent monitoring."[129] These cases of female homosexuality in his writings diverged more widely from ideas of bourgeois respectability than his middle- and upper-class male patients, with whom he developed amicable relations.[130] Furthermore, female homosexual patients did not seem to seek the respectability and acceptance from him that many male homosexuals—especially of the middle and upper classes— desired. From Krafft-Ebing's presentation of them, we surmise that most of the women were unwilling participants who cared little whether their desire was judged as immoral or perverse by their sexologist.

As Lang notes, this is why in the case of Krafft-Ebing it was hard for scholars to see the agency of homosexual women in relation to the medical discourse of the time.[131]

As degeneration and perversion were not regarded as gender-specific, Krafft-Ebing saw no reason to think that the number of male and female homosexuals would differ. He attributed the scarcity of female homosexual case vignettes to women's reluctance to openly confess due to the fact that female homosexuality was not criminalized in Germany, as it was in Austria. He also assumed that lesbians passed more easily as heterosexual in society on the assumption (not shared by Freud) that their sex drive was lower than men's. Nonetheless, he did try to include cases about women and lesbians in the ninth edition of *Psychopathia Sexualis*.[132]

Albert Moll and Freud

After the death of pioneer sexologists like Krafft-Ebing and the Italian physician Paolo Mantegazza (1831–1912), Moll, Hirschfeld, Ellis, and indeed Freud were the more influential sexologists during the early part of the twentieth century. While the legacy of Hirschfeld and Ellis have been discussed by scholars, Moll's work has been largely forgotten beyond the history of medicine, because it was entirely overshadowed by that of Freud. Moll's achievements were revealed by revisionist scholarship on the sexologists, and these are certainly of interest to historians of psychoanalysis; nonetheless, this should also not distract us from Freud's separate contribution.

Indeed, before Freud, Moll wrote about infant sexuality, the relationship between normal and abnormal sexuality, problems of the etiology of sexual pathologies, including degeneration, and the question of homosexuality. In Moll's *Libido Sexualis*, published in 1897, he went far beyond Krafft-Ebing and other sexologists as they were influenced by Morel's hypothesis of degeneration. For example, Moll assumed the latent homosexuality of "normal" individuals as well as the latent heterosexuality of homosexuals. He argued for the abolition of Paragraph 175 of the German penal code criminalizing homosexual acts; he thought a natural drive to procreation in humans was less noticeable in his time, and he discussed sexuality in children before puberty.[133]

The dispute about priority—"who explored things first"—and a strong personal animosity between Freud and Moll possibly stopped Freud from discussing Moll's work in great detail in 1905 in "Three Essays on the Theory of Sexuality."[134] In that publication, Freud briefly acknowledged his debt to the sexologists, but did so in broad strokes, effectively dismissing their detailed debates and terminology. In the first footnote of that text, he wrote:

> The accounts in the first treatise are extracted from the known publications by v. Krafft-Ebing, Moll, Moebius, Havelock Ellis, Näcke, v. Schrenk-Notzing [correctly: Schrenck-Notzing], Löwenfeld – Eulenburg, J. Bloch [correctly: I. Bloch] as well as the works in the *Jahrbuch für sexuelle Zwischenstufen* [*Yearbook for Sexual Intermediate Stages*], published by M. Hirschfeld. Since in these all the other literature on the topic is listed comprehensively, I could spare myself detailed references.[135]

Thus, as scholar (and leading sexologist in West Germany from the 1960s onwards) Volkmar Sigusch notes, although Freud mentioned Moll, he neither discussed his work *Libido Sexualis* in detail, nor the ideas of others.[136] Sigusch also notes, however, whatever influence Moll's earlier ideas and their personal rivalries and animosities may have had on Freud, there were substantial differences between them. During Freud's lifetime, Moll was a competitor who represented a sexology that focused on consciousness and behavior. In contrast, Freud's theories differed from sexology in terms of elements such as conscious and unconscious, internal fantasy and external reality, experience and behavior. Most sexologists could not accept that individuals were denied their own reason as Freud would have it.[137]

In addition, Moll's ideas on homosexuality were more reactionary than Freud's, as revealed in Moll's bitter and ugly dispute with Magnus Hirschfeld who, like Freud, challenged Moll's expertise in the field of sexuality. In reaction, Moll saw himself in contrast to Hirschfeld as a "pure scientist" working objectively in the pursuit of academic truth and uninfluenced by political or personal interests. He accused Hirschfeld of political agitation due to the latter's work under the motto of *per scientiam ad iustitiam* (Through Science to Justice) and his action on behalf of the first homosexual movement. Moll saw Hirschfeld's work as a reformer linking science with everyday life and his worldview in representing the Scientific-Humanitarian Committee (Wissenschaftlich-humanitäres Komitee) as unscientific. Moll may also have experienced a personal, homophobic rejection of Hirschfeld as "abnormal," unmanly, and effeminate, someone he thought incapable of unprejudiced study and treatment of patients who were sex offenders.[138]

Although Moll had signed the 1898 petition that Hirschfeld and the Scientific-Humanitarian Committee submitted to the German parliament, which envisaged legal equality of homo- and heterosexual acts between persons over the age of sixteen, by 1900 Moll started to undermine both Hirschfeld's and the Committee's work. In this he revealed his own conservatism vis-à-vis homosexuality. For example, Moll argued that individuals do not tend to perceive their own actions as pathological, suggesting that homosexuals' claim to always having felt as they did was unscientific; he also argued that the fact that something is natural does not mean it is necessarily healthy. From a medical point of view, the only question for Moll was whether homosexuality was hereditary or acquired. He added that treatment of homosexuality was necessary because in adults it was "a definitely pathological phenomenon."[139] To convert the homosexual sex drive, Moll proposed psychological treatments such as self-education and suggestion. At the same time, he believed there was no established treatment, and that in many cases it was advisable to refrain from treating homosexuality, but not the homosexual, who was "often enough not a healthy person in general."[140] In 1905, Moll attacked Hirschfeld more ferociously, especially with regard to homosexuality. As Sigusch explains,

> [Moll] called Hirschfeld's teachings "poison" for every homosexual who was interested in "cure," and was worried about the seduction of young men. He thought the "danger of breeding homosexuality ... much higher" than at the time when he had signed the petition of the Scientific-Humanitarian Committee.[141]

Moll accused the Committee of manipulating the findings of science and using the glorification of homosexuality as a tool. He opposed these tendencies as well as the assumption that something hereditary could not be changed.[142]

Freud, too, rejected the politics of Hirschfeld and homosexual activists who idealized only the fine characteristics of homosexuals. But his conclusions differed from Moll's. Freud did not seek treatment for homosexuality per se, he avoided the question that preoccupied Moll about whether homosexuality was hereditary or acquired, and he did not define homosexuality in adults as a pathological phenomenon, as discussed below.

Freud and Havelock Ellis

In his 1920 essay on female homosexuality, it seems that Freud was mostly in dialogue with Havelock Ellis (whose work, though still discussed, has been eclipsed by Freud's writings since the mid-twentieth century). Historian Ivan Dalley Crozier shows that the two men had considered each other's theories and utilized aspects of the other's work, but they were also careful not to appear to be following one another too closely. In 1897, Ellis believed that homosexuality was another manifestation of the sexual impulse as he conceived it—as neither sin nor sickness. Unlike Krafft-Ebing, Ellis did not hold a theory of different gradations of sexual type. Instead, he viewed homosexuality as either congenital or acquired, and as a common biological manifestation both in humans and in animals; this emphasis was often associated with Ellis. Ellis also believed that homosexuals simply had a different object of desire.[143] He, too, was a complex figure who was seen as a radical sexual reformer challenging the prevailing law against male homosexuality in England, and insisting that homosexuals had made important contributions to society. He was also an early supporter of the feminists.[144]

However, as historian Smith-Rosenberg has argued, the medical discourse and political realities pertaining to women's rights made what Ellis said about female homosexuality fundamentally different, imbued with conservative implications, as in his attacks upon the New Women whom he saw as sexually perverted and even socially dangerous. Although he was a humanist who advocated to protect male homosexuality from the law, insisting more clearly and directly than any writer that it was a congenital anomaly and therefore not degenerate, Ellis contended that a woman's love for other women was in itself sexual and "inverted." Ellis believed that a small percentage of lesbians were biologically and hereditarily inverted and unable to change their inclinations. He thought they should be socially tolerated and not harmed and that they posed no grounds for alarm. The more problematic group of women in his view were those he labelled as the "congenital invert"—that is, women who were not genetically inverted but who possessed a genetic predisposition for the advances of other women. Such acquired homosexuality was preventable and curable, he believed, and such women could become heterosexually "normal." As he conceptualized sex as part of a biological model that viewed reproduction in evolutionary Darwinian terms, inversion remained abnormal for Ellis. Although at first sympathetic to feminism, he believed that the feminists had gone too far and had become "unnatural" when the New Women remained unmarried, career-oriented, politically active, and often engaged in overly close loving ties in colleges or other institutions now open to women. As Ellis thought that women were by nature sexually passive, the female invert had to act like a man sexually and therefore she "unnaturally" inverted traditional femininity.[145]

In the 1905 publication in which Freud discussed sexual aberrations, we saw that he acknowledged his debt to the earlier writings of sexologists such as Krafft-Ebing, Moll, Schrenck-Notzing, and Hirschfeld. But it was Ellis's work, which Freud had read carefully, that held special significance for Freud's writing on sexuality. Freud used it to develop his ideas on how the sexual instinct relies partly on a sexual object for satisfaction, and he relied on Ellis's extension of Moll's work on the sexual impulse more than the original (also because of the antagonism between Freud and Moll). Yet simultaneously, and throughout the 1905 text, Freud presented a theory of sexual aberrations which was more complex than that of Ellis, as he developed and refined his ideas much further. Importantly, as we saw, Freud believed that there were two forms of sexual aberration, which he divided into the aberration of sexual aim and that of sexual object. Homosexuality belonged to the latter and, unlike Ellis, Freud eschewed the division into a congenital versus acquired etiology of inversion. Also unlike Ellis, Freud emphasized that all humans are bisexual though, as mentioned above, he did not support—indeed he was critical of—the third sex theories of Ulrichs and Hirschfeld.[146] Freud developed these 1905 views further in 1920 to distinguish himself from Ellis and his biological emphasis, and from the supporters of the third sex theory.

Freud's Contribution

Thus, perhaps in more ways than he himself admitted, Freud's ideas grew partly in dialogue with those of the sexologists whose views he advanced and refined. Nonetheless, he offered far greater scope than them in the form of an overarching treatment method and a much more psychological framework focusing on the individual rather than on statistically numerous case histories. Therefore, he was fundamentally able to challenge the sexological model in explaining homosexuality.[147] As historians Birgit Lang and Katie Sutton write, too, with the birth of psychoanalytic theory and Freud's rewriting of human sexual development in his 1905 essay, we can identify

the emergence of fundamentally new understandings of "sexual inversion" and its conceptual successors, "homosexuality" and "bisexuality." Freud understood these phenomena from a developmental perspective and argued: "When, therefore, any one has *become* a gross and manifest pervert, it would be more correct to say that he has *remained* one, for he exhibits a certain stage of *inhibited development.*" This paradigm shift in the understanding of sexuality away from a congenital model that saw homosexuality as a hereditary and constitutional predisposition had implications for theory, therapy and politics alike.[148]

We should note that the revisionist literature revealed that, over time, some sexologists presented more nuanced views about homosexuality as pathology or degeneration, and even about the congenital model. But overall, such quoted statements remain true. Freud differed from them even more in that he placed new emphasis on the influence of "repressed" homosexual desires, he developed theories out of the assumption of universal bisexuality, and further destabilized the sharp binary between those presumed to have been born heterosexuals and homosexuals. Freud established a way to depathologize homosexuality on much firmer ground than the sexologists.[149]

Although, like the sexologists, Freud connected female homosexuality with masculinity in 1920, he viewed masculinity first and foremost as a psychological attitude, as noted above. His psychological explanation was more thorough than that of the sexologists who initially grounded homosexuality predominantly in biology before opening up—some more, others less—to psychological explanations too. Furthermore, though the sexologists gradually emphasized physiology less, they might still have expected confirmed homosexuals to show physical characteristics of the opposite sex.[150] Freud emphasized the more biological version of their views and, by contrast, reminded his 1920 readers that this was not unique to homosexuals—subjects from both sexes could manifest a degree of physical hermaphroditism. Furthermore, he noted that although the girl he discussed in his 1920 case was resolutely homosexual, she showed no significant deviation from the feminine physical type, nor any menstrual disturbance. It is true, Freud noted, the girl had her father's tall figure, her facial features were sharp, and she had an intellectual, lucid objectivity—traits which might be regarded as masculine. But he dismissed these distinctions as conventional rather than scientific. More important to him were the girl's aforementioned masculine behavior and psychology towards her beloved.[151]

Freud's views developed in part out of the ideas of the sexologists, but sexology was only part of the history of psychoanalysis, which also borrowed from other psychological models of the mind, as well as from literature and linguistics.[152] Through free association and dream analysis, psychoanalysis tried to offer patients a reconstruction of their psychic lives. The scope was far greater than that of the sexologists who, although they used patient accounts, remained closer in their aspirations to the natural sciences, and described many different occurrences of sexual behaviors in the form of natural history rather than developing an overarching treatment method or framework for understanding different aspects of humanity.[153]

Can the 1920 case of this young woman's homosexuality be labeled a late-acquired inversion, as most sexologists would have claimed? Freud sharply dismissed this as an overly simple solution to the question of homosexuality. While sexologists like Ellis categorized cases of homosexuality as congenital/innate and acquired/late-acquired, in 1920 (even more than in 1905) Freud wanted to eliminate this question altogether. He believed that the patient's sexual and psychological history revealed just how "fruitless and inapposite" congenital or acquired homosexuality was.[154]

Freud repeatedly rebuffed any negative view of her homosexuality per se and returned to analyzing her mental rather than her physical disposition. He also respected her feminism on its own grounds and not as a deviant transgression. Freud rejected the idea that *any* girl who suffered Oedipal disappointment would subsequently turn to homosexuality; that was merely one possible psychological solution. Asking his readers, by implication, to suspend judgment, he insisted in 1920, as before, that "even in a normal person it takes a certain time before the decision in regard to the sex of the love-object is finally made."[155] It remained unclear whether he was open to the idea that, as the girl had suffered from Oedipal disappointment and also from a marked masculinity complex since childhood, perhaps part of this acquired disposition (if it really was acquired) should be ascribed to an inborn constitution. But overall Freud wanted to steer clear of the question of nature versus nurture. He did so by presenting the sexologists as focusing too much on congenital constitution and then ignoring the ways in which they subsequently advanced to more nuanced views. Thus, in the 1920 analysis, he persistently argued for "a continual mingling and blending of what in theory we should try to separate into a pair of opposites—namely, inherited and acquired characters."[156] He presented sexological theory more simplistically than the extent to which it had already developed, but he also refined it further saying that it "would be best not to attach too much value to this way of stating the problem."[157]

This conclusion led Freud to strongly criticize the prevailing medical (and by this point also popular) term "inversion." He presented this idea, common among sexologists, to mean primarily physical inversion and that helped him to pit his ideas squarely against theirs as he insisted instead on a more psychological model. Furthermore, in his 1920 paper, Freud wished to intervene against the sexologists' literature on homosexuality, which he saw as failing to distinguish clearly between the choice of love-object, on the one hand, and the sexual characteristics and attitude of the subject, on the other. Freud mockingly protested that homosexuality was by no means as simple as commonly depicted by sexologists (in his rigidly biological interpretation of their work): a physical inversion where "a masculine mind, irresistibly attracted by women, but, alas! imprisoned in a feminine body."[158] Instead, he insisted, as he developed his 1905 ideas further, it was a question of three sets of characteristics, namely physical sexual characteristics (returning to the possibility of physical hermaphroditism), mental sexual characteristics (a masculine or feminine attitude rather than biology), and the object choice. He maintained that to some extent these varied independently of one another, and manifested in different individuals in a diverse range of permutations.[159] Thus, while object choice remained a definitive element of homosexuality, as Freud had argued in 1905, in 1920 he restated the correlation of object choice with homosexuality by expanding it and distancing himself from any singular definition in favor of one central element among the three sets of characteristics.[160] Freud further developed his 1905 rewriting of human sexuality more clearly and broadly in 1920, presenting an understanding of sexual inversion according to a developmental model that downplayed the question of heredity or degeneracy even more than in the writings of the sexologists, despite their development of more nuanced ideas. He persisted in this vein even when sexologists such as Hirschfeld and Ellis continued to argue that homosexuality could be "caused" by hereditary factors—though that did not necessarily make it degenerate or pathological—and when they promoted predominantly congenital models while still insisting on the health of homosexual people.[161]

To summarize this section on Freud and the sexologists, I have identified a variety of ideas that pre-dated Freud or arose during his lifetime. Freud participated in the medical and sexological literature and borrowed his ideas in part from the contributions of others (while only cursorily acknowledging his debts). We now have better and more nuanced accounts of the work of key early sexologists. The picture that emerges if we integrate this revisionist literature with the discussion of psychoanalysis is that Freud may have been less unique and groundbreaking in his views on sexuality. There are similarities and parallels between his ideas and those of others. At the same time, however, we should not ignore the differences, or his direct intervention in the field, or the innovation that was still part of his contribution that remained radical and immensely open-minded for his time.[162]

Other Psychoanalysts' Work on Homosexuality

Freud's thoughts on homosexuality in 1920 also differed from those of other psychoanalysts up until then, and it is worth looking at this briefly. His 1905 statements that homosexuality was a result of a developmental inhibition, or a fixed incomplete state of development stemming from universal bisexuality rather than hereditary or degenerative perversions, enabled and opened up other psychoanalytic explorations of homosexuality before his 1920 essay.[163]

For example, Sándor Ferenczi in Budapest expanded on Freud's connection of homosexuality with paranoia in the latter's 1915 interpretation of Daniel Paul Schreber's *Memoirs of My Nervous Illness* (1903). Freud explored the delusional outcomes of rejecting male homosexual desire and argued that there was a close link between paranoia and homosexuality. Similar insights had also appeared in his 1910 biographical study of Leonardo da Vinci, in which Freud expanded his initial etiological explanation of male homosexuality from 1905, emphasizing factors such as narcissism, an eroticized early relationship with the mother, and an absent or insignificant father. He also argued that a heterosexual object choice did not extinguish earlier homosexual tendencies, it simply forced them out of the sexual realm and transformed them into contributing an erotic element to friendship and comradeship, to *esprit de corps*, and to the love of mankind in general. As Lang and Sutton stressed too, before 1920 and the postwar period these theoretical suggestions in themselves "removed discussions of homosexuality from an explanatory framework of pathological degeneration or inborn constitutional predisposition."[164]

Thus, in 1912, Ferenczi—who was sympathetic to the homosexual activist movement—decided to advance Freud's views and argued that the paranoid mechanism was a specific reaction to a homosexual object choice, claiming that paranoia in general is a distorted form of homosexuality. Two years later, in 1914, Ferenczi described a more feminine, passive brand of male invert and individuals who expressed a wish to be women as suffering from a "developmental anomaly" likely to be congenital. He believed that psychoanalysis could not offer them a cure, only relieve their neurotic symptoms. In contrast, he categorized masculine, active homosexuals attracted to younger or more feminine men as being under compulsion neurosis, believing that these men who are often averse to women may be amenable to psychoanalytic therapy. At the same time, he believed that psychoanalysis was unlikely to remove the homosexual attraction altogether, but rather that it would replace it with a form of bisexuality, or reawaken the men's attraction to women.[165]

Wilhelm Stekel, writing from Vienna in 1912, developed Freud's idea of universal bisexuality to describe repressed homosexuality. He argued, for example, that frustrated homosexual desires could explain the precocious behaviors of female prostitutes and nymphomaniacs. He was also more conservative in his thinking than other psychoanalysts and retreated to sexological views of inversion in his description of transvestism as an expression of repressed homosexuality.

Perhaps the prewar figure most removed from Freud's progressive views was Isidor Sadger who wrote extensively on homosexuality in 1908, but unlike Freud attempted to treat, normalize, and "cure" homosexual patients. Sadger believed that psychoanalysis had the unique potential to achieve a cure and shift the invert's behavior and, more importantly, their sexual ideal which was not inborn but rather developed over time. He believed that he could achieve the first psychoanalytic cure of a seemingly pure male invert and make him heterosexual. Sadger also claimed that the path to homosexuality was developed through narcissism and the love of one's own self or ego. Analyst Otto Rank developed this idea, unusually in relation to female homosexuality, in a 1911 essay in which he argued that narcissistic female patients had an unconscious inverted tendency arising from a repressed fixation on the mother.

Unlike Freud, whose theories even had emancipatory potential for homosexuals due to his emphasis on curing his patient's neurosis rather than their homosexuality, other analysts, like some sexologists, tried to cure the homosexuals themselves, or viewed them through the lens of pathology. In 1920, Freud used Margarethe Csonka's life to exemplify the psychological mechanism underlying her particular object choice, and did so much more clearly than he had before the war. Unlike Sadger, Freud did not aim to cure the girl but rather to explore with her the complex road towards a same-sex sexual object. Throughout his meetings with this self-identifying homosexual woman, he challenged his patient and the expectations of his readers.[166] Thus, even in relation to other psychoanalysts, Freud's insistence in 1920 on the need to separate an individual's homosexuality from their need for therapy stood out as unusually nonjudgmental and nonnormative.[167]

It was mostly after the First World War, and after Freud had published his 1920 case, that a more intense and in-depth exploration of female homosexuality occurred, together with a significant shift away from the discussion of male to female homosexuality. In the 1920s, female patients came to dominate the writing of male psychoanalysts such as Freud, Stekel, Sadger, and Ernest Jones who were then joined by female analysts such as Joan Riviere, Helene Deutsch, Sylvia Payne, and others.[168] Prior to that, the discussion of female homosexuality can be seen as a somewhat forgotten aspect of debates on women's sexuality more broadly.[169]

After the Second World War, some psychoanalysts maintained Freud's nonjudgmental approach to homosexuality. But others adopted more conservative views that ranged from seeking a cure to outright homophobia against sexual minorities.[170]

Should Psychoanalysts Treat Homosexuality?

We saw that some sexologists were gradually moving away from the idea that homosexuality was pathological; but for Freud, as noted, this was the starting point. In the 1920 text, he presents a clear resistance to the idea of treatment for homosexuality and, moreover, to seeing it as a problem. He assigned a limited role to treatment, thereby boldly rejecting "conversion therapies" for homosexuals. He even stated, "It is not for psycho-analysis to solve the problem of homosexuality."[171]

So, what was the role of psychoanalysis vis-à-vis homosexuality for Freud in 1920? His answer was highly restrained and radical: it was only to disclose the psychical mechanisms that resulted in determining the object choice of love, and to trace back the paths from them to the instinctual dispositions in the patient. There the work of psychoanalysis ended, according to Freud, and the rest was left to future biological research, about which he was skeptical. Freud clarified that psychoanalysis had a common basis with biology, presupposing an original bisexuality in human beings. "But psycho-analysis cannot elucidate the intrinsic nature of what in conventional or in biological phraseology is termed 'masculine' and 'feminine': it simply takes over the two concepts and makes them the foundation of its work."[172]

Freud questioned his role as the analyst of a young woman who neither believed herself ill nor complained of her condition, and whom he himself did not consider hysterical or suffering from a neurotic conflict. Furthermore, rather like the direction other sexologists were taking more hesitantly, he strongly doubted the ability of treatment to convert one variety of the genital organization of sexuality (such as homosexuality) into the other (heterosexuality). In the 1920 text, he broadened his statements on this topic.

Why then should an analyst take on such a case? Freud's radical answer was that he did not promise the parents that the girl could be changed; he merely pledged his willingness to study her carefully. A favorable prognosis for therapy and change could exist, he added, only where there were considerable signs of a heterosexual choice of object, that is, in a still-oscillating or definitively lasting, bisexual organization.[173] Success in such an analysis would be limited and consist only in gaining access to the opposite sex (which had hitherto been barred to the homosexual), thus restoring his or her full bisexual functions. Freud was hoping at most to make her open up to her initial bisexuality rather than abandon any chosen object of sexual desire. Yet, progressively for his time and among his contemporaries, Freud emphasized that thereafter it lay solely with the patient to choose whether or not to abandon the path banned by society.[174] In assigning psychoanalysis such a confined role, and homosexuals the right of choice for their own lives, Freud's 1920 paper was particularly radical for his time and revealed a more impartial and unbiased attitude to homosexuality.[175]

Freud's views on homosexuality in this paper are also relevant to discussions of the role of the male expert vis-à-vis female homosexuals, a topic covered much less by other sexologists. Freud's writing on analytic technique shed some light on his own limitations as an analyst of young women. As the girl did not feel any urgent need to be freed from her homosexuality, it is not surprising that Freud terminated the analysis early. The reason for this, he theorized, was that the girl was limited in her ability to form a positive transference towards him as a male analyst. Behind her pretended consideration for her parents and willingness to make the attempt to be transformed, he thought, lay an attitude of defiance and revenge against her father which held her fast to her homosexuality. Thus, Freud decided to break off the treatment and advised her parents that it should be continued by a woman doctor.

Yet Freud's failure to complete the treatment of an earlier patient, Dora, also aged eighteen, whose homosexuality towards a Frau K Freud mostly ignored, seems to resemble some of the dyadic dynamics of the 1920 case. As Jacqueline Rose argues, it is tempting to see the Dora case as anticipating the paper on female homosexuality in "the insistence of Dora's desire for Frau K. as substitute for the absent mother in the case ... the nature of the preoedipal attachment between mother and girl child, an attachment Freud finally makes specific to feminine sexuality in its persistence and difficulty." Rose further argues that, in 1920, Freud acknowledged the homosexual factor in all feminine sexuality, which was to lead to his revision of his theories of the Oedipus complex for the girl.[176] Indeed, for all the reasons discussed, we should also think of the 1920 paper as an often-forgotten element in the interwar femininity debate, for there he also discussed female sexuality generally, beyond reproduction, and the possibility of a homosexual choice for women.[177]

Freud the Jewish Man and Female Homosexuality

What role did the fact that Freud was writing his conceptualization of homosexuality in an antisemitic society play? Different Jewish studies scholars have shown how much the ideas of Freud as a Jewish man were produced in response to the antisemitic, racial, and homophobic medical views of the turn of the century. Daniel Boyarin shows how this context influenced Freud's 1890 shift away from his so-called seduction theory to the Oedipus complex. This, claimed Boyarin, was a move from the theory of hysteria that accommodated male hysteria and homoeroticism towards a more heterosexual, if not heterosexist, active, and phallic conceptual framework. It was based on an anxiety stemming from the pathologizing of homosexuality and the prevailing antisemitic racialization of the Jews. Thus, Freud was wary about the ideational connections formed in the antisemitic, homophobic discussions at the time between hysteria, effeminacy, passivity, pathology, homosexuality, and Jewishness.[178] Freud wanted to ensure that psychoanalysis would not be remembered as a "Jewish science," and that his theories would be seen as universal, as Steven Frosh argued.[179] Sander Gilman convincingly showed the extent to which Freud's work emerged in the context of racist rhetoric and imagery. Gilman revealed, for example, that as Jews were seen as circumcised, effeminate, and analogous to women during the fin-de-siècle period, in Viennese slang the clitoris was known as the "Jew" and female masturbation as "playing with the Jew." Freud responded to this association of femininity with the Jewish male by reversing it and seeing the clitoris, the "Jew," as a sign of masculinity. He stressed that in order to achieve mature adult femininity, the masturbatory clitoris (that is the "Jew," the masculine) must be abandoned.[180] Overall, Gilman's work helps to explain how Freud projected onto women some of the antisemitic and homophobic images of Jewish men. This insight led Ronnie Lesser to wonder: "Could a Jewish man even be in a position to depathologize homosexuality without risking that he himself would be seen as fitting the stereotype of a feminine, homosexual Jew?"[181]

My answer to this question in the present book, which emphasizes the radical sides of Freud, suggests that it could be a complicated "yes." Besides worrying about the racial and homophobic associations that pervaded effeminacy, homosexuality, and Jewishness and thus moving to a phallocentric, Oedipal sexual theory (in ways that were therefore also problematic and came at a price), Freud was also paradoxically remarkably open, curious, and indeed radical in his attitude towards homosexuality.[182] His universal axiom that all human beings are bisexual meant that homosexual desire was a universal experience, even for those who "matured" to heterosexuality.

Freud insisted that homosexuals were different but not ill, so his argument was partly analogous to what he wanted to believe about Jewishness. In his theories, he was able to counter the stigma of racism and pathology by making the perverse and the marginal normal and universal. Thus, Jews and homosexuals were not degenerate, congenitally pathological, or ill.[183] Following his encounter with Margarethe Csonka, he openly declared that his female homosexual patient was neither neurotic nor hysterical in any way, and assigned an unusually restrictive role to treatment that did not see her homosexual choice as a problem in itself. Freud presented an alternative view to that of the sexologists that opened up ways of thinking about female homosexuality beyond pathology, heredity, or degeneracy.[184] The plot thickens further if we add the fact that his young female patient was an assimilated Jewish homosexual who had found her own sources of resistance against her antisemitic and homophobic culture and society, at times also adopting some of Freud's own ideas.

Notes

1 See John Forrester, "If p, Then What? Thinking in Cases," *History of the Human Sciences* 9, no. 1 (1996): 1–25.
2 See the section titled "Freud and the Sexologists."
3 Arnold I. Davidson, "How to Do the History of Psychoanalysis: A Reading of Freud's 'Three Essays on the Theory of Sexuality,'" *Critical Inquiry* 13, no. 2 (1987): 252–277.
4 As argued by Birgit Lang and Katie Sutton, "The Queer Cases of Psychoanalysis: Rethinking the Scientific Study of Homosexuality, 1890s–1920s," *German History* 34, no. 3 (September 2016): 420–423.
5 Forrester, "If p, Then What?" 3. As Lang notes, the collective genre of the case study compilation has received little critical attention. It can be seen as a mixture of academic discourse and case vignettes aiming to be empirical. In *Psychopathia Sexualis*, the key sexological text by Richard

von Krafft-Ebing, his expert discourse employed a neutral voice, sometimes forging medical vocabulary, and exploring new phenomena and disorders. Birgit Lang, "Normal Enough? Krafft-Ebing, Freud, and Homosexuality," *History of the Human Sciences* 34, no. 2 (2021): 93. See also P. Savoia, "Sexual Science and Self-Narrative: Epistemology and Narrative Technologies of the Self Between Krafft-Ebing and Freud," *History of the Human Sciences* 23, no. 5 (2010): 17–41; B. Lang, J. Damousi, and A. Lewis, *A History of the Case Study: Sexology, Psychoanalysis, Literature* (Manchester: Manchester University Press, 2017); I. Dalley Crozier, "Pillow Talk: Credibility, Trust and the Sexological Case History," *History of Science* 46, no. 4 (2008): 375–404.

6   Forrester, "If p, Then What?" 10. See also Anne Sealey, "The Strange Case of the Freudian Case History: The Role of Long Case Histories in the Development of Psychoanalysis," *History of the Human Sciences* 24, no. 1 (2011): 36–50.

7   As argued by Lang and Sutton, "The Queer Cases," 423–425. See also Michal Shapira, "'Speaking Kleinian': Susan Isaacs as Ursula Wise and the Inter-War Popularisation of Psychoanalysis," *Medical History* 61, no. 4 (October 2017): 525–547. For a critique of the psychoanalytic case study in psychoanalysis and masking in part methodological shortcomings, see Frank J. Sulloway, "Reassessing Freud's Case Histories: The Social Construction of Psychoanalysis," *Isis* 82 (1991): 245–275, esp. 246.

8   Forrester, "If p, Then What?" 10. On the same page, Forrester added "So psychoanalytic discourse combines two unlikely features: it promises a new way of telling a life in the 20th century, a new form for the specific and unique facts that make that person's life their life; and at the same time, it attempts to render that way of telling a life public, of making it scientific. The bridge between these two aims is the case-history, along with the curious and distinctive narratives of transference and counter-transference phenomena that increasingly came to dominate 'clinical writing', as it is called."

9   Sigmund Freud, "Fragment of an Analysis of a Case of Hysteria," *The Standard Edition of the Complete Psychological Works of Sigmund Freud*, ed. J. Strachey (London: Hogarth Press, 1920), vol. 7 (1905), 1–122. From here on, *The Standard Edition* is referred to as *SE* with the volume number, date and page number(s) only.

10 Sigmund Freud, "Notes upon a Case of Obsessional Neurosis," *SE* vol. 10 (1909), 151–318.

11 Sigmund Freud, "Analysis of a Phobia in a Five-Year-Old Boy," *SE* vol. 10 (1909), 1–150.

12 Sigmund Freud, "Psycho-Analytic Notes on an Autobiographical Account of a Case of Paranoia (Dementia Paranoides)," *SE* vol. 12 (1911), 1–82.

13 Sigmund Freud, "From the History of an Infantile Neurosis," *SE* vol. 17 (1911), 1–124.

14 Sealey, "The Strange Case," 36–37.

15 Ibid., 39–41. See also Carol Berkenkotter, *Patient Tales: Case Histories and the Uses of Narrative in Psychiatry* (Columbia: University of South Carolina Press, 2008).

16 Sealey, "The Strange Case," 41–42.

17   Ibid., 42.

18   Ibid., 43.

19   Ibid., 43; cf. Sulloway, "Reassessing Freud's Case Histories."

20   Sealey, "The Strange Case," 43–44, 47.

21   On the development of case histories in the history of medicine, see Jan Goldstein, *Hysteria Complicated by Ecstasy: The Case of Nanette Leroux* (Princeton, NJ and Oxford: Princeton University Press, 2011).

22   Sigmund Freud, "The Psychogenesis of a Case of Homosexuality in a Woman," *SE* vol. 18, 147.

23   This is the spelling in the Strachey translation of *coquette.*

24   Freud, "The Psychogenesis," 147.

25   Ibid., 148.

26   Ibid. In the winter of 1918–1919, Freud and his family still suffered from the dire conditions and limited resources prevailing in postwar Vienna. Freud had to ask for food, cigars and clothes from family members and friends abroad. Throughout the war, Freud worried about his enlisted sons, but in a tragic and devastating blow, he lost his daughter Sophie to the postwar Spanish influenza in January 1920. By February 1920, the resourceful Freud was able to repay his benefactors with the help of money he received for treating American and English patients. And, by December 1921, he felt comfortable enough to receive visitors again in his now-heated home. See Peter Gay, *Freud: A Life for Our Time* (New York: Norton, 2006), 361–390. According to Jones, Freud completed writing the text in German in January 1920 and published it in March; see Ernest Jones, *Sigmund Freud Life and Work*, vol. 3: *The Last Phase 1919–1939* (London: Hogarth Press, 1957), 47:1–45. For more discussion on the war context, see Part II.

27   Jones, *Sigmund Freud Life and Work*, 149.

28   Ibid., 155–160.

29   Freud, "Three Essays on the Theory of Sexuality," *SE*, vol. 7 (1905), 123–246; Sander L. Gilman, *Freud, Race, and Gender* (Princeton, NJ: Princeton University Press, 1993), 135–136; Freud, "The Psychogenesis," 150. See the full discussion in the section on "The Sexologists."

30   S. Flanders, F. Ladame, A. Carlsberg, P. Heymanns, D. Naziri, and D. Panitz, "On the Subject of Homosexuality: What Freud Said," *International Journal of Psychoanalysis* 97, no. 3 (2016): 933–950.

31   My thanks to Doron Halutz for insisting that I pay full attention to this point.

32   See Carol Smith-Rosenberg, *Disorderly Conduct: Visions of Gender in Victorian America* (New York: Oxford University Press, 1985), 245–286; Martha Vicinus, *Intimate Friends: Women Who Loved Women, 1778–1929* (Chicago: University of Chicago Press, 2004), 203–204, and the section on "Freud and The Sexologists."

33   Flanders et al., "On the Subject," 933–950. In later essays, Freud used the word "perversion" but with reservations; see Flanders et al., "On the Subject," 941–945; Freud, "Three Essays," 123–246. See also Heike Bauer, "Theorizing Female Inversion: Sexology, Discipline, and Gender at the Fin de Siècle," *Journal of the History of Sexuality* 18, no. 1 (2009): 84–102.

34   Freud, "Three Essays," 135–136,

35   Ibid., 149.
36   Ibid., 150.
37   Ibid., 149–162.
38   Ibid., 137.
39   Ibid., 139.
40   Ibid., 140.
41   Ibid., 144–148.
42   George Chauncey, "From Sexual Inversion to Homosexuality: Medicine and the Changing Conceptualization of Female Deviance," *Salmagundi* 58/59 (1982): 114–146.
43   Havelock Ellis, "Sexual Inversion in Women," *Alienist and Neurologist* 16 (1895): 141–158.
44   Chauncey, "From Sexual Inversion," 123.
45   Ibid., 137. Chauncey claims that Freud "reintroduced the acquired theory of homosexuality so forcibly that congenital theories such as Ellis's were completed to devote much of their later work to his refutation."
46   My discussion of Freud's different views on homosexuality in this and the subsequent two paragraphs is based on Flanders et al., "On the Subject," 933–950.
47   Flanders et al., "On the Subject," 934.
48   Ibid. In his later essay, "Some Psychical Consequences of the Anatomical Distinction between the Sexes" (1925), Freud argued forcefully that "all human individuals, as a result of their bisexual disposition and of cross-inheritance, combine in themselves both masculine and feminine characteristics, so that pure masculinity and femininity remain theoretical constructions of uncertain content." Quoted in Flanders et al., "On the Subject," 935. See the original in Sigmund Freud, "Some Psychical Consequences of the Anatomical Distinction between the Sexes," *SE* vol. 19 (1925), 258.
49   Flanders et al., "On the Subject," 934, 935–936. Freud, "The Psychogenesis," 151, 157, 171.
50   Freud, "Three Essays," 145. See Flanders et al., "On the Subject," 937; Freud, "Analysis of a Phobia in a Five-Year-Old Boy," 109–110.
51   Quoted in Flanders et al., "On the Subject," 937. See original in Freud, "Three Essays," 145. See also Sigmund Freud, "Leonardo da Vinci and a Memory of his Childhood," *SE*, vol. 11 (1910), 57–138.
52   Flanders et al., "On the Subject," 939. See the original in Sigmund Freud, "On Narcissism: An Introduction," *SE*, vol. 14 (1914), 67–102.
53   See, for example, Freud, "Psycho-analytic Notes on an Autobiographical Account of a Case of Paranoia," and later Sigmund Freud, "Some Neurotic Mechanisms in Jealousy, Paranoia and Homosexuality," *SE*, vol. 18 (1922).
54   Flanders et al., "On the Subject," 940. See the original in Sigmund Freud, "Female Sexuality," *SE*, vol. 21 (1931), 229–230, and Freud, "The Psychogenesis," 169. Later, in 1931, he argued that the disparagement of a woman "regarded as castrated" can lead her to "cling with defiant self-assertiveness to her threatened masculinity. To an incredibly late age she clings to the hope of getting a penis some time. That hope becomes her life's aim; and the phantasy of being a man in spite of

everything often persists as a formative factor over long periods." This "masculinity complex" in women can—though it does not necessarily—result in a homosexual choice of object. Such women experience a narcissistic injury stemming in part from their recognition of themselves as socially lacking. See Freud, "Female Sexuality," 229–230.

55 Flanders et al., "On the Subject," 941.

56 Quoted in Flanders et al., "On the Subject," 944. See the original in Freud, "The Psychogenesis," 158. Flanders et al. conclude that although the language of developmental arrest is sustained throughout Freud's writings on homosexuality, it is important to recall that Freud remained circumspect regarding the very achievement of final normal sexuality as the route to adult heterosexuality. He saw it as outwardly complex, full of predicaments, and also shaped and enforced by the demands of civilization and the pressure to reproduce in order to ensure the continuity of society. He even assumed in 1905 that, without social pressure, many more people would adopt homosexuality. In 1919, he stressed that the path towards adult sexuality is rarely straightforward and told his readers that they must reckon with the possibility that something in the nature of the sexual instinct itself is unfavorable to the realization of complete satisfaction in civilization. See Flanders et al., "On the Subject," 945, 949. Flanders et al. also point out another theme in Freud's writings regarding homosexuality, which they relate to aggression and destructiveness and which is less relevant perhaps to the 1920 case. In 1910, Freud noted that future inverts pass through a phase of very intense but short-lived fixation on a woman, and put themselves in the role of the mother as a parent to gain some mastery over the situation of dependency (before choosing a narcissistic solution). In 1922, Freud looked at the function of aggression arising out of strong attachment in the development of boys. The boy's rivals (in the form of other boys) can become objects of intense hatred that, through repression, are turned into objects of desire. While Freud was always concerned with hatred, after 1920 and the introduction of the death drive, his focus became more pronounced. In 1923, he theorized that there was an element of aggression left over after the ego managed to give up its objects. In giving up the erotic attachment, there was always something left over as free aggression circulating in the psyche and not bound by sublimation or identification or an object relation. See Flanders et al., "On the Subject," 945–949.

57 Sigmund Freud, "Letter to an American Mother," *American Journal of Psychiatry* 107 (1951): 787. Freud was more open towards homosexuality than many of his psychoanalytic followers. See Michal Shapira, *The War Inside: Psychoanalysis, Total War, and the Making of the Democratic Self in Postwar Britain* (New York: Cambridge University Press, 2013), chap. 6; Dagmar Herzog, *Cold War Freud: Psychoanalysis in an Age of Catastrophes* (Cambridge University Press, 2016), chap. 2; Anita Kurimay, *Queer Budapest, 1873–1961* (University of Chicago Press, 2020), chap. 3.

58 See more on the antisemitic/homophobic context of this later in Part I.

59 In 1920, in the case of women, unlike men, we shall see that he retained the view that the girl had partly inverted male character behavior. See also Chauncey, "From Sexual Inversion," 124–125.

60 Ibid., 133.
61 Teresa de Lauretis and Elisabeth Young-Bruehl, "Introduction," in *That Obscure Subject of Desire: Freud's Female Homosexual Revisited*, ed. Ronnie C. Lesser and Erica Schoenberg (New York: Routledge, 1999), 6–7.
62 See Gilman, *Freud, Race, and Gender*, 136; Lang and Sutton, "The Queer Cases," 439.
63 Lang and Sutton, "The Queer Cases," 437.
64 Ibid., 438–439, 443.
65 Freud, "The Psychogenesis," 156.
66 Ibid., 157.
67 Ibid., 158.
68 Ibid., 158.
69 Ibid.
70 Ibid., 159.
71 Other historical same-sex couples did so as well; see Vicinus, *Intimate Friends*. Cf. Sharon Marcus, *Between Women: Friendship, Desire, and Marriage in Victorian England* (Princeton, NJ and Oxford: Princeton University Press, 2007).
72 On this, see Gay, *Freud*, 507–511.
73 Freud, "The Psychogenesis," 161.
74 Ibid., 161. Upper-middle-class feminists were also campaigning against prostitution and for the "rescue" of these women. See Judith R. Walkowitz, *City of Dreadful Delight: Narratives of Sexual Danger in Late-Victorian London* (Chicago: University of Chicago Press, 1992).
75 Freud, "The Psychogenesis," 154.
76 Ibid., 169. Cf. a different explanation in Freud, "Some Psychical Consequences of the Anatomical Distinctions," 253, in which he saw the girl who disavowed castration as insisting on "being like a man." Cf. also the explanation he provides in Freud, "Female Sexuality," 130, that homosexuality is the result of an identification with the phallic mother, as suggested in Anne Worthington, *Female Homosexuality: Psychoanalysis and Queer Theory* (PhD diss., London: Middlesex University, 2011).
77 Johan H.W. Van Ophuijsen, "Contributions to the Masculinity Complex in Women," *International Journal of Psychoanalysis* 5 (1924): 39–49.
78 See Lang and Sutton, "The Queer Cases," for more on their differences. On their similarities, see Lang, "Normal Enough?" 90–122.
79 See Gay, *Freud*, 120.
80 Freud's presentation of his work against a less nuanced version of the work of others, it seems, has also contributed to the more one-dimensional manner in which the sexologists were seen afterwards, and overshadowed them.
81 Harry Oosterhuis, "Sexual Modernity in the Works of Richard von Krafft-Ebing and Albert Moll," *Medical History* 56, no. 2 (April 2012): 133–155; Harry Oosterhuis, *Stepchildren of Nature: Krafft-Ebing, Psychiatry, and the Making of Sexual Identity* (Chicago: University of Chicago Press, 2000). See also Volkmar Sigusch, "The Sexologist Albert Moll: Between Sigmund Freud and Magnus Hirschfeld," *Medical History* 56, no. 2 (2012): 184–200; Lutz D.H. Sauerteig, "Loss of Innocence: Albert Moll, Sigmund Freud and the Invention of Childhood Sexuality

Around 1900," *Medical History* 56, no. 2 (2012): 156–183. Cf. Frank Sulloway, *Freud, Biologist of the Mind: Beyond the Psychoanalytic Legend* (New York: Basic Books, 1979), 277–320.

82 Oosterhuis, "Sexual Modernity," 133–155.

83 We can see Lang and Sutton as supporting this view in "The Queer Cases." And early on see George Chauncey, "From Sexual Inversion."

84 Bauer, "Theorizing Female Inversion," 85. Viennese-born human rights activist Karl Maria Kertbeny first coined the word "homosexuality" in 1868; see Lang and Sutton, "The Queer Cases," 419.

85 Bauer, "Theorizing Female Inversion," 87–92; Lang and Sutton, "The Queer Cases," 419.

86 Ibid.; Robert Beachy, "The German Invention of Homosexuality," *The Journal of Modern History* 82, no. 4 (2010): 801–838.

87 Oosterhuis, "Sexual Modernity," 137–138. See also Oosterhuis, *Stepchildren of Nature*, 37–72; Jeffrey Weeks, *Coming Out: Homosexual Politics in Britain, from the Nineteenth Century to the Present* (London: Quartet Books, 1977), 1–22.

88 Oosterhuis, "Sexual Modernity," 135.

89 Bauer, "Theorizing Female Inversion," 87–92.

90 For a reading that claims that sexology pathologized friendships between women, see the classic account by Lillian Faderman, *Surpassing the Love of Men: Romantic Friendship and Love between Women from the Renaissance to the Present* (London: Junction, 1981). For an inquiry of female same-sex manifestations before and beyond the sexological accounts and terminology, see Marcus, *Between Women*. For the development of lesbian culture in the interwar period, see Laura Doan, *Fashioning Sapphism: The Origins of a Modern Lesbian Culture* (New York: Columbia University Press, 2000).

91 Bauer, "Theorizing Female Inversion," 85. Cf. Claudia Breger, "Feminine Masculinities: Scientific and Literary Representations of 'Female Inversion' at the Turn of the Twentieth Century," *Journal of the History of Sexuality* 14, nos. 1–2 (2005): 76–106.

92 Richard von Krafft-Ebing, *Psychopathia Sexualis: Eine klinisch-forensische Studie*, 1st edn (Stuttgart: Enke, 1886); Bauer, "Theorizing Female Inversion," 94.

93 Quoted in Bauer, "Theorizing Female Inversion," 94.

94 Ibid., 94–96.

95 Ibid., 96–97. See also Robert Beachy, *Gay Berlin: Birthplace of a Modern Identity* (New York: Knopf, 2014); M.M. Lybeck, *Desiring Emancipation: New Women and Homosexuality in Germany, 1890–1933* (New York: State University of New York Press, 2014); Katie Sutton, *Sex Between Body and Mind: Psychoanalysis and Sexology in the German-Speaking World, 1890s-1930s* (Ann Arbor: University of Michigan Press, 2020).

96 Smith-Rosenberg, *Disorderly Conduct*, 270.

97 This paragraph and the quotations are taken from Smith-Rosenberg, *Disorderly Conduct*, 270.

98 Ibid., 271.

99 Quoted in ibid., 272.

100 Ibid., 265–267,

101 Oosterhuis, "Sexual Modernity," 136–138. See also Benjamin Kahan, *The Book of Minor Perverts: Sexology, Etiology, and the Emergences of Sexuality* (Chicago: University of Chicago Press, 2019).
102 Oosterhuis, "Sexual Modernity," 136–138. See also Harry Oosterhuis, "Richard von Krafft-Ebing's 'Step-Children of Nature': Psychiatry and the Making of Homosexual Identity," in Vernon A. Rosario, ed., *Science and Homosexualities* (New York: Routledge, 1997).
103 Oosterhuis, "Richard von Krafft-Ebing's 'Step-Children,'" 68.
104 As Oosterhuis suggests, "By naming and classifying virtually all non-productive sexuality, he was one of the first to synthesize medical knowledge of what was then labeled 'sexual perversion.'" Oosterhuis, "Richard von Krafft-Ebing's 'Step-Children,'" 70.
105 Ibid., 71.
106 Gay, *Freud*, 120.
107 Oosterhuis, "Richard von Krafft-Ebing's 'Step-Children,'" 72–74.
108 Ibid., 82.
109 Ibid., 75–82.
110 Albert Moll's thinking on sexual matters also shifted, especially with regard to homosexuality. Before the First World War, he was open-minded and pragmatic for his time. However, in contrast to Krafft-Ebing, Moll later became more conservative and nationalistic, and even turned against Hirschfeld and his Scientific Humanitarian Committee, which he had earlier supported. Moll criticized Hirschfeld and his supporters for promoting homosexual emancipation and the popularization of sexual knowledge by mixing scientific sexology with a leftist polemical agenda. Moll's work—despite the publication of English translations of *Das Sexualleben des Kindes* in 1912 and of *Untersuchungen über die Libido sexualis* in 1933—was largely forgotten in the English-speaking world. Oosterhuis, too, speculates that this was probably because his work was overshadowed by Freud's theories. See Oosterhuis, "Sexual Modernity," 136–137. Oosterhuis writes: "In his book on the *Libido Sexualis* (*Untersuchungen über die Libido sexualis*), Moll elaborated the most comprehensive and sophisticated general theory on sexuality before Freud wrote his *Drei Abhandlungen zur Sexualtheorie* (1905) ("Three Essays on the Theory of Sexuality") and before Havelock Ellis completed his monumental *Studies in the Psychology of Sex (1897–1910)*. Whereas systematic classification of deviant sexualities formed the leading principle of Krafft-Ebing's *Psychopathia Sexualis,* Moll's book on *Libido Sexualis* was organized on the basis of an explanatory framework of sexuality in general, and his discussion of perversion served as a supportive elucidation. His sexual theory was completed with the publication of *Das Sexualleben des Kindes* in 1908 [*The Sexual Life of the Child*]," 136. More information on Moll is included in the subsequent discussion.
111 As claimed by Oosterhuis in "Sexual Modernity," 142–143.
112 Ibid., 145.
113 Ibid., 146–147.
114 Oosterhuis, "Richard von Krafft-Ebing's 'Step-Children,'" 85.
115 Oosterhuis in "Sexual Modernity," 146–147.

116 Ibid., 147. From this, Oosterhuis infers, "it was only a small step" to Freud's 1905 conceptualization of "lusting 'libido' and 'pleasure principle', according to which the sexual desire's only built-in aim is its own satisfaction." Indeed, this acknowledgment that sexual desire and variation are not directly tied to reproduction is central to the modern sexual ethos. But I suggest that Freud developed his ideas beyond those of the sexologists in ways that were significant. Ibid., 148.

117 Ibid., 148–150.

118 Ibid.

119 Ibid.

120 Lang, "Normal Enough?" 92.

121 Oosterhuis, "Richard von Krafft-Ebing's 'Step-Children,'" 85.

122 Lang et al., *A History of the Case Study*, 73–78.

123 Lang, "Normal Enough?" 94.

124 It is also interesting to note that Freud criticized the early politics of homosexuals who presented homosexuality in ideal terms. He was more careful than Krafft-Ebing, who was willing to print the words of those who wrote to him and idealized homosexuals throughout history. Freud was also more cautious than Magnus Hirschfeld who tried to present homosexuals as respectable. In contrast, Freud was interested in a universal model of sexuality with all its messiness and less idealized forms. In 1917, he even stated that "of course [homosexuals] are not, as they also like to assert, an 'élite' of mankind; there are at least as many inferior and useless individuals among them as there are among those of a different sexual kind." See Lang, "Normal Enough?" 101. See also the references she provides: G. Makari, *Revolution in Mind: The Creation of Psychoanalysis* (New York: HarperCollins, 2008), 114; Sutton, *Sex Between Body and Mind*, 78.

125 Lang, "Normal Enough?" 107.

126 Cf. Ibid.

127 Oosterhuis, "Sexual Modernity," 133–155.

128 Lang, "Normal Enough?" 96–97.

129 Quoted in ibid., 97.

130 Ibid.

131 Ibid., 98. See also Faderman, *Surpassing the Love of Men*; Chiara Beccalossi, *Female Sexual Inversion: Same-Sex Desires in Italian and British Sexology, c. 1870–1920* (New York: Palgrave Macmillan, 2012); Rebecca Jennings, *A Lesbian History of Britain: Love and Sex Between Women Since 1500* (Santa Barbara, CA: Greenwood World, 2007).

132 Lang, "Normal Enough?" 99.

133 Volkmar Sigusch, "The Sexologist Albert Moll," 184–186, 189.

134 Ibid., 188–191.

135 Quoted with the additions in brackets in Sigusch, "The Sexologist Albert Moll," 188.

136 Ibid.

137 Ibid., 191

138 Ibid., 192–193.

139 Quoted in Sigusch, "The Sexologist Albert Moll," 194.

140 Quoted in and based on ibid.

141 Ibid., 195.

142 Ibid., 195–196. As Hirschfeld was being persecuted by antisemitism and fled to Paris to escape the Nazis, Moll in a horrific act wrote a damning letter intended to prevent Hirschfeld from establishing himself in exile in France, where he died in 1935. Moll, too, eventually was treated as a "Jewish doctor" in accordance with the Nazis' racial laws, and he died impoverished on the same day as his rival Sigmund Freud in 1939. See Sigusch, "The Sexologist Albert Moll," 197–200.

143 Ivan Dalley Crozier, "Taking Prisoners: Havelock Ellis, Sigmund Freud, and the Construction of Homosexuality, 1897–1951," *Social History of Medicine* 13, no. 3 (2000): 450–454. On the psychological development of the Oedipus complex in women, see Freud, "Female Sexuality," 221–244.

144 See also Ivan Dalley Crozier, "The Medical Construction of Homosexuality and its Relation to the Law in Nineteenth-Century England," *Medical History* 45, no. 1 (2001): 61–82.

145 Smith-Rosenberg, *Disorderly Conduct*, 276–279. In her influential and by now classic reading of women's writing in the 1920s, Smith-Rosenberg claimed that, at the time, the new generation of feminists became less successful in their tactics as they adopted the medical and male language of female inversion associated with anti-feminist stereotypes. This language caricatured the New Woman as "inverted" because she was seen to follow mannish pursuits, such as wearing trousers or smoking. In contrast, revisionist readings on this topic, such as those of Heike Bauer, suggest that that the existence of the "feminist invert" enabled a new understanding whereby women could theorize sex and gender beyond scientific taxonomies, and make affirmative use of a notion of female masculinity. For Bauer, female inversion was an affirmative part of a new feminist politics as the New Women understood gender in terms of binaries that could be reversed and refuted. At the same time, she claims, because their affirmative politics of female inversion was understood as a form of rational female masculinity, and because it challenged the existing gender order, it marginalized same-sex desire. The women understood the notion of female inversion not in terms of sexual identity but as a refutation of sex-gender binaries. This again came at a price, because as a result they downgraded female same-sex desire. See Bauer, "Theorizing Female Inversion," 99–102. It is interesting to consider that Freud's 1920 female patient was a feminist who saw herself thinking about same-sex desire beyond the scientific taxonomy, and that this was a plausible historical possibility open to her. She did not simply mean to challenge gender identities but sought a place for her sexual identity and desire too.

146 See the full discussion of their differences and similarities in Dalley Crozier, "Taking Prisoners," 454–455. See the psychological development of the Oedipus complex for women in Freud, "Female Sexuality."

147 Dalley Crozier, "Taking Prisoners," 456, 464; Lang and Sutton, "The Queer Cases," 423.

148 Lang and Sutton, "The Queer Cases," 419–420; emphasis in the original. They quote from Freud, "Fragment of an Analysis," 1–122, esp. 50.

149 Cf. the slightly different emphasis in these statements borrowed from Lang and Sutton, "The Queer Cases," 420.

150 For further discussion of their nuanced views, see Smith-Rosenberg, *Disorderly Conduct*, 245–286. See also Phyllis Grosskurth, *Havelock*

Ellis: A Biography (Toronto, ON: McClelland and Stewart, 1980); Chris Waters, "Havelock Ellis, Sigmund Freud and the State: Discourses of Homosexual Identity in Interwar Britain," in *Sexology in Culture: Labelling Bodies and Desires*, ed. Lucy Bland and Laura Doan (Chicago: University of Chicago Press, 1998).

151   Freud, "The Psychogenesis," 154. See Dalley Crozier, "Taking Prisoners," 451–452 (449–456).

152   Dalley Crozier, "Taking Prisoners," 453.

153   Ibid., 456, 464.

154   Freud, "The Psychogenesis," 154. See Dalley Crozier, "Taking Prisoners," 451–452 (449–456).

155   Freud, "The Psychogenesis," 154.

156   Ibid., 169.

157   Ibid., 170.

158   Ibid. Here Freud is perhaps writing teasingly against the ideas of Ulrichs, transposing them to the context of female inversion. Krafft-Ebing thought of female inversion as an inborn, contrary, sexual feeling in women, but he also emphasized that same-sex feeling was not necessarily a form of physiological inversion. See Bauer, "Theorizing Female Inversion," 90–97. In 1905, Freud had already written against this idea, saying: "The theory of bisexuality has been expressed in its crudest form by a spokesman of the male inverts: 'a feminine brain in a masculine body'. But we are ignorant of what characterizes a feminine brain. There is neither need nor justification for replacing the psychological problem by the anatomical one. Krafft-Ebing's attempted explanation seems to be more exactly framed than that of Ulrichs but does not differ from it in essentials. According to Krafft-Ebing (1895, 5), every individual's bisexual disposition endows him with masculine and feminine brain centres as well as with somatic organs of sex; these centres develop only at puberty, for the most part under the influence of the sex-gland, which is independent of them in the original disposition. But what has just been said of masculine and feminine brains applies equally to masculine and feminine 'centres'; and incidentally we have not even any grounds for assuming that certain areas of the brain ('centres') are set aside for the functions of sex, as is the case, for instance, with those of speech." Freud, "Three Essays," 142–143.

159   Freud, "The Psychogenesis," 170.

160   Flanders et al., "On the Subject of Homosexuality," 938. The roots of that are found in 1905 in Freud, "Three Essays," 135–148.

161   Lang and Sutton, "The Queer Cases," 419; Smith-Rosenberg, *Disorderly Conduct*, 245–286.

162   As Dagmar Herzog wrote: "Freud's work was full of contradictory impulses and recurrent self-amendments, but he was unquestionably more open and curious about the intricacies of desire than many of the psychoanalysts who followed in his wake. On the one hand, there were in Freud's published work the normative assumptions that what he called 'a normal sexual life' required: making an object choice external to the self; connecting the drive for pleasure to reproductive aims; fusing component instincts and putting any remaining partial (polymorphous, oral, anal) drives into the service of genital primacy. On the other hand, there

were also in his published writings repeated declarations that: homosexuals were not necessarily any more mentally unstable than heterosexuals; homosexuals could in fact serve as analysts themselves; and
there was as little prospect of converting homosexuals to heterosexuality
as the reverse." Herzog, *Cold War Freud*, 58. See also Tim Dean and
Christopher Lane, *Homosexuality and Psychoanalysis* (Chicago: University of Chicago Press, 2001); Diana Fuss, ed., "Pink Freud," Special
Issue of *GLQ: A Journal of Lesbian and Gay Studies* 2 (1995).

163   My discussion of the period leading up to 1920 and of this particular
point is entirely based on the work of Lang and Sutton, "The Queer
Cases," 425–437. See also Makari, *Revolution in Mind*, 93–97, 112–113,
219.

164   Lang and Sutton, "The Queer Cases," 425.

165   Ibid., 428–429; Freud, "Psycho-Analytic Notes on an Autobiographical
Account," 1911–1913.

166   Lang and Sutton, "The Queer Cases," 429–444.

167   Ibid., 442.

168   Ibid., 437, 441; Shapira, "Criticizing Phallocentrism," 1–24.

169   Shapira, "Criticizing Phallocentrism."

170   On this there is much to say that has been explored elsewhere. See
Michal Shapira, *The War Inside*, chaps. 5 and 6; Herzog, *Cold War
Freud*, chap. 2.

171   Freud, "The Psychogenesis," 171.

172   Ibid.

173   Ibid., 151.

174   Ibid.

175   Rose also briefly noted that in the 1920 article Freud was "in a way at
his most radical, rejecting the concept of cure, insisting that the most
psychoanalysis can do is restore the original bisexual disposition of the
patient, defining homosexuality as nonneurotic." Jacqueline Rose,
Sexuality in the Field of Vision (New York: Verso, 1986), 35.

176   Rose, *Sexuality in the Field of Vision*, 35.

177   See Russell Grigg, *Female Sexuality: The Early Psychoanalytic Controversies*, ed. Dominique Hecq and Craig Edward Smith (New York:
Other Press, 1999). The 1920 case is not included in this collection.

178   Daniel Boyarin, "Freud's Baby, Fliess's Maybe: Homophobia, Anti-
Semitism, and the Invention of Oedipus," *Gay and Lesbian Quarterly* 1
(April 1995): 115–147.

179   Steven Frosh, *Hate and the "Jewish Science": Anti-Semitism, Nazism and
Psychoanalysis* (New York: Palgrave Macmillan, 2005).

180   Gilman, *Freud, Race*, 39–40.

181   Lesser, "Introduction," 6; cf. 1–9.

182   Boyarin, "Freud's Baby"; Herzog, *Cold War Freud*, 58.

183   Gilman, *Freud, Race*, 136–137.

184   Lang and Sutton, "The Queer Cases," 438–439, 443.

Part II: Margarethe Csonka/ Sidonie Csillag (1900–1999)

An Assimilated Jewish Female Homosexual in Modern Vienna

Despite the fact that the 1920 case was relatively obscure, a new biography has revealed the young woman to be Margarethe (nicknamed Gretl) Csonka whose married name was Trautenegg. The authors of the biography, however, gave her a pseudonym of their choice: Sidonie (or Sidi) Csillag,[1] at Csonka's request for a more aesthetic name.[2] Since using the pseudonym perpetuates her obscurity, I will use her real name in what follows. I will also add historical detail to reveal her side of the story and background, and further information on her family and her beloved.[3] While the biography offers important facts and her testimony, I will add historical details and provide an analysis of these facts, crafting a different, opposing narrative by Csonka as she rejected Freud's scientific discourse and, as noted in Part I, drew on the model of heterosexual romantic love and beyond.

Part II is divided into three sections that broaden the context of the encounter between Freud and Csonka, and deepen our understanding of the cultural and historical conditions that prevailed alongside the medical-sexological debates of the time. The first focuses on Csonka's story from the point of view of the new opportunities emerging for women, partly as a result of urban developments, in the changing modern city of Vienna. The second section investigates the differences between Freud and Csonka's narratives; it emphasizes Csonka's active role in the analysis and in her own life, and shows how she borrowed from romantic cultural rather than medical codes of behavior. The third section explores changes that were taking place in Jewish life at the time and how these influenced Csonka, as well as Freud, and opened both to new prospects and predicaments. I will show how, as an assimilated Jewish woman, Csonka took advantage of the developing modern city that offered new freedoms for women and Jews, despite the rising antisemitism. These three sections will situate Csonka as an active character in the social, urban, cultural, and ethnic

DOI: 10.4324/9781003352662-3

changes of twentieth-century Vienna, thereby further illuminating the diverse ways of understanding homosexual female desire and love beyond the confines of medical circles.

Same-Sex Love and the Rebuilding of the City of Vienna: Margarethe Csonka Meets Leonie von Puttkamer

The locations in which Margarethe Csonka and her beloved met offer a fine view of modern Vienna and its middle- and upper-class rituals in the early twentieth century. I will argue that the changing city not only presented a historical background to the one-sided love story, but it also actively enabled its progression, and served as a catalyst for the two women to take advantage of the new possibilities opening up to them.[4]

Margarethe, or Gretl, first met her flamboyant beloved, whom we now know was the Baroness Leonie von Puttkamer (1891–1953), in a resort outside Vienna, in the summer of 1917 during the First World War, when Gretl was seventeen. As her older brother had been drafted into the military, and her father was away taking care of his paraffin oil business, which was essential to the war effort, Gretl was sent to a vacation resort in Semmering with her younger brother and a governess. Gretl was mostly protected from the horrors of the war, but as the supply situation in Vienna deteriorated, she frequently witnessed unpleasant scenes and was glad to spend the summer in the luxurious Grand Hotel Panhans (still operating today[5]) where Vienna's and Budapest's high society, the nouveau riche, and wartime profiteers vacationed. Strolling around the hotel with a friend of the same age, Gretl encountered two women walking arm in arm, occasionally in the company of an older man. One of these was Leonie von Puttkamer, from an old noble Prussian family that had fallen into financial difficulties. Gretl's friend explained that their governess's disapproval was due to the fact that the two women were lovers. Gretl found comfort in this as she understood that she might not be the only woman to love women.[6]

Following the mysterious Leonie back to the city of Vienna, Gretl saw that she got off at the Kettenbrückengasse station and that she lived in one of the modern upper-class Linke Wienzeile buildings, a landmark in the city. The Wienzeile (Vienna Row) was a street created between 1899 and 1905 by channeling the Wien River; regulations pertaining to the riverbanks resulted in a division between the Rechte Wienzeile (right-hand Vienna Row) and the Linke Wienzeile (left-hand Vienna Row). The buildings, which were celebrated residential

Figure 1 Margarethe Csonka as a young woman
Source: Freud Museum archive, Vienna, Sigmund-Freud-Privatstiftung.

Figure 2 Leonie von Puttkamer, 1919
Source: Freud Museum archive, Vienna, Sigmund-Freud-Privatstiftung.[7]

dwellings built by the famous Austrian architect, designer, urban planner, and modern theorist Otto Wagner, were a remarkable example of the revolutionary new Vienna Secession style (Wiener Secession). With the completion in 1898–1899 of the apartment houses on the corner of Linke Wienzeile and Klöstergasse, Wagner was said to have created "a piece of architectural history"—the buildings are considered to be among the most elaborate examples of art nouveau architecture in Vienna.[8] In order to understand the significance of these and other urban sites, including modern phone booths, trains, markets, and cafés to the two women's meetings, relationship, and the ability to move around town, it is worth digressing into the details of key architectural and design changes taking place in Vienna between the mid-nineteenth and early twentieth centuries, for they were creating new options for these two modern yet very different women.

Modernized Vienna: Urban Development Brings New Opportunities

New behaviors and ways of being were not only being opened up by the prevailing medical, sexological, and psychoanalytic discourse but also by the construction of new urban spaces in which the women's independence and same-sex relationship encountered new possibilities. Thus, the fruits of modern urbanity in the city of Vienna are another way of making sense of what was possible for Gretl and Leonie beyond the medical discourse. These changes, and the background to them, provide a fuller picture of the times and environment in which Csonka, Puttkamer, and Freud lived. In my analysis of Margarethe Csonka's life and her meetings with her beloved, the innovations of Otto Wagner play a central role. The extensive changes in Vienna and the explosion of new ideas in urban planning and design influenced and expanded the opportunities available to the men and women living in, strolling, and moving around the city.

The background to these changes began in the mid-nineteenth century when, from the 1860s, the urban landscape underwent an extensive transformation.[9] The key site of construction was the Ringstrasse—the famous main circular boulevard separating the historic Innere Stadt (old town) from the rest of Vienna. After the city walls were dismantled in 1857, the ring road was built on the site of the medieval city's fortifications. It comprised a complex of large public buildings and private dwellings with a stylistic homogeneity and scale.

From the 1860s to 1890s, many buildings were constructed along the Ringstrasse in the so-called historicist style—an eclectic use of former components of classical, Gothic, Renaissance, and Baroque architecture. These new buildings represented the values of the liberals who had taken control. As historian Carl Schorske famously argued, the liberal city fathers took pride in transforming the city's face and projected their image of stability and reason onto space and stone; the emphasis in style was not on utility or function but on beautifying the city's image. In the age of revolution and counter-revolution in the 1840s and 1850s, the Austrian army favored the construction of a broad boulevard to maximize the mobility of troops and to minimize the possibility of barricades. But with the liberals' takeover, the plan for the Ringstrasse was changed to reflect the peaceful values of the new ruling class, to represent the new sense of law and order, and to offer embellishment through art rather than military force. Centers of constitutional government and higher culture came to dominate the Ringstrasse; the new plan created circular flow and cut off the old center from the new suburbs. New regulations in 1859 also established full freedom of trade thereby helping the city's economy to grow rapidly, and with it the city's population. The middle-class liberals emphasized their independence from the past in terms of law and science, but in architecture they expressed their values in a contradictory manner by retreating into history and choosing to build monumental public buildings. In terms of residences, the Ringstrasse houses marked a transitional state: stylistically they still integrated commercial space with domestic housing, but the commercial sector was rarely the workplace of those who lived in the buildings. Homes in the Ringstrasse were also a good investment: the highest social strata in Vienna chose not only to reside in but also to own the buildings of the Ring. These were considered secure assets as high aristocrats, merchants, widows of fixed income, doctors, and university professors could buy the whole building and live in one unit while earning an income from the others. Thus, at a reasonable cost, the Ringstrasse residential buildings combined social desirability and maximum profit-making grandeur.[10]

Towards the end of the nineteenth century and as intellectuals began raising doubts about the culture of liberalism, critics such as Otto Wagner concentrated their attacks on the Ringstrasse style and era, and he was eventually able to build some of the key spaces in which the women met and befriended one another. The Ringstraßenstil (ring road style) was seen as a self-confident, stable, central symbol for Austrians—perhaps similar to the significance of Victorianism for the English. The Ringstrasse, therefore, became a site criticized by a new generation of architects as part of a broader critique of the fathers of liberalism by their so-called symbolic sons, expressed in terms of architectural questions and aesthetic criticism. As Schorske argued, those who perceived a dissonance in the relationship between style and function in the Ringstrasse were raising a broader question about the relationship between cultural aspirations and social content in a liberal bourgeois society. This discrepancy between style and content appeared on both sides of the map: from those with more conservative leanings and those who espoused a more modern forward-looking approach. Among the former was architect Camillo Sitte, a planner who took the historic and aesthetic aspirations of the Ringstrasse builders seriously; therefore his main point was to criticize what he saw as the neglect of this tradition in favor of the needs of modern life. On the opposing side was Otto Wagner, who in contrast to Sitte believed that the Ringstrasse era represented the ideas of the past socially and aesthetically in ways that were becoming less relevant, and he denounced the disguise of modernity and its functions behind the stylistic presentation of history. Thus, writes Schorske, in the battle around the Ringstrasse, both ancients and moderns attacked the synthesis of the mid-century Ringstrasse builders. Sitte presented archaism and Wagner spoke of functional futurism, but both fed a new aesthetics of city building in which social aims were influenced by psychological considerations of what would be a suitable style for the new modern urban individual.[11] Sitte's critiques were imbued with nostalgia for a vanished past; for him the Ringstrasse represented a heartless utilitarian rationalization, or what he termed "the rage of open state," that isolated both humans and buildings. His solution was to create squares that would allow for human communications rather than the traffic-dominated space. He was also enthusiastic about the art of the pre-industrial past and the old artisanal and craft culture that were indeed under threat and in slow decline.[12] By contrast, Wagner, who won the competition for a new development plan for Vienna in 1893 and who had the final say, had a different vision, which became relevant to our understanding of Freud's 1920 case of female homosexuality and the city in which he, his patient, and her beloved operated. In 1894, Wagner addressed his audience at the Viennese Academy of Fine Arts saying:

> Art and artists should and must represent their times. Our future salvation cannot consist in mimicking all the stylistic tendencies that occurred during the last decades ... Art in its nascence must be imbued by the realism of our times.[13]

Instead of expanding historicism to redeem modern man from modern technology and utility, as Sitte wanted, Wagner sought to tone down historicism and to emphasize instead the values of a rational urban civilization. In contrast with Sitte's views, however, for Wagner the Ringstrasse was not utilitarian or modern enough. Wagner called upon architects and city planners to look further into the future, beyond the Ringstrasse era, and to envisage a more democratic approach that included the technical and scientific achievements of the day combined with the practical character and demands of modernity. Thus, he sought new aesthetic forms to express the hectic capitalist urbanity that he wholeheartedly supported and embraced, both as an architect and urban theorist.[14] Freud's approach, too, could be said to be modern, for example in his willingness to accommodate the way his patients felt and thought about their lives, moving away from the constraints of the past towards realizing their aspirations in the present. It was within this tension between modernity and the past that the two women, Margarethe Csonka and Baroness Leonie von Puttkamer, behaved in the city and in their lives more generally. Gretl was seeking to break free of her family's past, and her parents' (especially her father's) conservative and bourgeois attitudes. Leonie had broken with her family's former nobility and carved out a definitively anti-conservative and anti-bourgeois existence and lifestyle.

A little more historical context on Wagner will illuminate the changes in the times and the city spaces that were occurring at the time. As a young architect, Wagner participated in the development of the Ring and the historicist style. During the first stage of his career until roughly 1887, he was largely influenced by the historicist tradition, and he characterized his own style as a "certain free Renaissance."[15] The gradual change began around 1886, when Wagner built the so-called Villa Wagner I to which he attached two panels on the main façade. One stated "Sine arte sine amore non est vita" (There is No Life Without Art and Without Love), and the other "Artis sola domina necessitas" (The Sole Mistress of Art is Necessity). These two mottos announced the change that characterized Wagner's future work, uniting beauty and functionality. In 1895, even in Villa 1 that was built mostly in the free Renaissance style, he changed the right-hand pergola into a billiard room, and, in 1899, he converted the left-hand pergola into a studio. The latter showed Wagner's turn towards a new style as it was adorned by art nouveau stained glass windows designed by the painter Adolf Böhm. Wagner's break with the past was even more clearly expressed in his 1896 manifesto *Modern Architecture*, in which he declared "something impractical cannot be beautiful." He added, "the upheaval will prove so violent, that we will hardly be able to speak of a Renaissance of the Renaissance." Instead, he believed that there would be "a complete new rebirth"; the architect must aspire to establish new forms or improve any form that can accommodate modern construction and needs.[16] This new spirit of change and possibility, and the ability to reimagine life in a modern vision of transgressing past patterns, was something that Gretl and Leonie (each in their different circumstances) must have shared. Out of necessity and desire, each broke away from the history of her family's older generations and embraced the new opportunities offered by modern Vienna. Both could be said to be modern women seeking practical solutions to their problems. For Leonie this meant having to make a living after her parents fell into financial difficulties and so she chose prostitution in the city, but she could also have affairs with both men and women, travel around town and have access to its different exclusive and less exclusive urban spaces. Gretl was practical in her pursuit of same-sex love so she embraced the new opportunities to walk and commute around town, access different modern sites and eventually even her meetings with Freud that allowed her to escape from her parents' home and some of their values.

Wagner emerged as a functional theorist and builder through his 1890s involvement with urban engineering projects and through his openness to the secessionist art movement that was part of Vienna's art nouveau. These helped him to develop an intellectual critique that would further transform Vienna and its people into the 1920s and beyond.[17] In 1892–1893, Wagner won one of two first prizes in the competition for Vienna's General Regulatory plan, which led to his subsequent appointment as a General Planner. Thus, Wagner became a central influencer concerned with city planning in the broadest sense. This included the construction of the municipal railway (Stadtbahn) between 1894 and 1900, the Danube canal construction in 1894 and 1896–1899, as well as the future development of the city. In the early municipal railway buildings of the belt and suburban line built in 1894 and 1897, Wagner retained simple forms related to the style of the Renaissance. But, by contrast, in the Lower Vienna Valley and the Danube Canal line stations, art nouveau style was applied with organic structural ornamentation made of stucco and forged iron.[18] In his role as a chief architect of the construction of the Vienna city railroad system in 1894–1901, Wagner was responsible for the execution of all planning and production down to the fine details, including the architectural design of the collective overhead and underground configurations including rails and guards. He was also in charge of the furnishing and lighting, logistics of the baggage room, construction of elevators, and installation of technical engineering. He was involved with designing viaducts, large tunnels, and bridges. In short, it was one of the largest engineering construction projects of the early twentieth century and for many architects and historians it became the embodiment of modernity itself; it brought new prospects for Viennese men and women and new ways for them to traverse and move around the city.[19] One can imagine how women, taking advantage of the new systems of transport that enhanced their mobility across the city, might also have enjoyed the beautifully decorative art nouveau aesthetic that prevailed in these new constructions. The municipal railway was also Vienna's largest construction project at the time. Wagner was able to oversee the construction of some thirty railway stations as well as 45 kilometers of track. Some of the stations were particularly elaborate in design and attracted attention. Karlsplatz station, close to where Margarethe Csonka and the Baroness Leonie von Puttkamer would walk, is a case in point. Built and decorated in the art nouveau style, it had a visible iron skeletal structure with white marble slabs and corrugated sheet iron displaying new industrial realism (usually reserved for industrial architecture).[20] Wagner wanted to design stations representing both simplicity and utility. He strove to harmonize art and purpose, believing that together they offered the best modern solution, and he attempted to celebrate the technological as a culture in its own right. Wagner stressed the primacy of utility overall and the importance of adapting to purpose over form, but he did so without abandoning the idea of the architect as artist. While Sitte saw the architect's role as celebrating beauty rather than utility, Wager wanted to serve utility as an aesthetic good that was the best fit for modern life. In his critique of the architecture of his time, Wagner argued that it did not keep pace with social change and relied too much on historical styles rather than expressing modern man's needs and outlook.[21] We shall see in what ways his statements also applied to women and their needs.

Looking for a visual style to fit the modern age, Wagner found part of the answer in the Wiener Secession and he became a member in 1899. Backed by a young group of artists and intellectuals, the secessionists formed a forward-looking art movement committed to breaking away from the historicist tradition and realism, to embrace a more internationalist view of art nouveau while combining artistic fields. They wanted to eradicate the perceived boundaries between fine and applied arts. The artists, sculptors, and architects chiefly associated with the secessionist style included Gustav Klimt, Koloman Moser, and Josef Hoffmann. The group's main goal was to create a "total art" that would unite architecture and decorative art, and depart from the more conservative historicists and classicism of the official Vienna Academy of Fine Arts, the Viennese Künstlerhaus, and the formal art salons.[22] They can be seen as a coalition of relatively progressive painters, architects, and designers, and Otto Wagner played a crucial role in bridging the gap between historicism and later developments. Nonetheless, Wagner remained attached to the idea that every new style grows out of the one that preceded it, and that new forms of construction, materials, and needs produce new creations. He wrote, "The point of departure of every artistic creation must be the need, the capacity, the means and the qualities of 'our' time."[23] The secessionists did not endorse a particular stylistic mode, as the issue was not only one of style but of quality of life. Thus, unlike smaller modernist art groups such as Der Blaue Reiter and Die Brücke in Germany, or Picasso's circle in France, the secessionists were primarily concerned with controlling the circumstances under which art was created, and with the right to create art freely. "We recognize no difference between high art and low art," the secessionists declared in their official magazine *Ver Sacrum* (*Sacred Spring*). "All art is good."[24] They offered innovative visual representations across artistic disciplines. Their motto, announced by Wagner's student, Joseph Maria Olbrich, was "To the Age Its Art, to Art Its Freedom." The co-founder and the first president of the secessionists, Gustav Klimt, influenced Wagner's ideas too, and provided him with a visual language to replace the historical styles of the Ringstrasse. Yet Wagner turned away from Klimt's internal psychological search and emphasis on the instinctual and erotic life presented in his paintings, and emphasized instead modernity as efficient and rational. At the center of Wagner's vision of modernity, as Schorske explains, was "an urban man with little time, lots of money, and a taste for the monumental." In his fast-moving world of time and motion, "painful uncertainty" was all too easily felt, and the architect had to overcome it by providing lines of movement. For this Wagner turned to Klimt's two-dimensional concept of space in his paintings to create a new way of building walls. Instead of the pronounced indented walls of the Ringstrasse Mietpalast in Wagner's first secessionist-style apartment house, the façade was built flat to represent its function as a wall (in ways that the Bauhaus would later develop further). The typical Ringstrasse house was differentiated from the street, but Wagner's secessionist front reflected the street's simplicity and submitted to and reinforced its direction. In his interiors, too, Wagner adapted the art nouveau line so that stair rails, carpets, and parquet floors were designed with decorated strips emphasizing direction and movement to help to overcome any modern psychological uncertainty. Indeed, Wagner influenced and contributed to an age of change and opportunity for individuals of diverse gender, religious, and ethnic histories; a time when people like Gretl and Leonie, from different classes, genders, and backgrounds, could meet and socialize in new ways in the rebuilt city.[25] This is explicated below where we see the impact of class, family, and gender on the circumstances in which the two women lived.

Wagner had a school of followers and exerted strong influence on his pupils at the Academy of Fine Arts in Vienna. They included the aforementioned Joseph Maria Olbrich and Josef Hoffmann as well as Karl Ehn, Jože Plečnik, and Max Fabiani. Thus, in trying to liberate art from the style of the past, the secessionist movement provided Wagner with a new anti-historical ornamental language. Wagner aimed to separate structure from style as part of his assault on the Ringstrasse architecture. For him, what was beautiful remained on the surface of the building as a cover to ornament its functional forms.[26] This architectural background also helped to facilitate meetings like those between Gretl and Leonie. The new artistic styles represented fresh ways of thinking beyond the past that must have imbued them with a sense of new adventure and possibilities for life.

The Linke Wienzeile and Other Modern Sites Around Town

Leonie von Puttkamer, as mentioned above, lived in one of the modern apartment houses of the Linke Wienzeile. Understanding the social and cultural meaning of these buildings helps to tie them to the analysis of the case. Wagner had a particular interest in the living conditions of modern people; his vision of modern man was of a citizen of big cities whose daily life was increasingly influenced by mechanization, and who participated with greater intensity in cultural life. Wagner joined in the trend of investing in profitable apartment buildings, both as owner and architect. His business model was to gain capital from the sale of the apartment houses in order to fund his next project.[27] With around fifty residences, it was his largest residential project before 1900.[28]

The building complex where Leonie von Puttkamer lived was arranged as three structures comprising a unified hub on a strategic corner of Linke Wienzeile 38–40 and Köstlergasse 1, close to the Naschmarkt. The large Majolikahaus was at Linke Wienzeile 40, and its entrance faced the boulevard almost opposite the Kettenbrück-engasse station that Csonka used. The building was paneled entirely with ornamental majolica tiles, creating colorful floral swirls of pink. The façades of the other two structures were ornamentally designed in plaster. Together they are some of the most celebrated buildings in Vienna for their artistic creativity and their provocation to conservative society. They remain striking for their color and art nouveau style.[29] This provocation against the prevailing conventions was an apposite backdrop to the life that Leonie von Puttkamer had chosen for herself. Similarly, Csonka would also thumb her nose at her family history and values in order to live the life she wanted.

Wagner divided the floors in an optimal layout and installed elevators with highly decorated iron gates in the secessionist style, and equipped the residents with bathrooms and stoves. In Wagner's own small model apartment that he called "a night lodging" he did not include a salon or library, but he did include a controversial glass bathtub composed of a nickel-plated metal frame construction in which the four crystal glass panels were held together. It seems to represent a tension between the aesthetics of transparency, the ethos of purity and hygiene, and the display of the erotic (with the latter perhaps of least importance). The buildings quickly gained a reputation as "the quintessence of modern, cosmopolitan living style."[30]

In order to stress functionality, Wagner eschewed the integration of commerce and domicile behind a unifying Renaissance front. Instead, the façade of the Wienzeile buildings were decorated with distinct, contrasting forms that reflected the two functions of the space within—that is, business below and residence above. A strip of glass and iron marked the ground floor as a commercial space, while on the second story the façade marked the residential function where the ornamentation also began. The ornamentation at the top included a luxurious little loggia with art nouveau swags, sprays, urns, and statues that marked the building as "a symbol of the urbane life of luxury that could have its economic basis in the prosaic, rational offices below."[31] Thus, the buildings revealed a dichotomous symbolization of their two functions. In Schorske's words,

> Wagner expressed the two sides of modern urban man as he saw him, each side in its own stylistic idiom: the man of business and the man of taste. Thus, he laid bare in precarious but open juxtaposition what the Ringstrasse architects had tried to integrate by concealment when … they screened commercial functions in the residential style of the Renaissance palace.[32]

The Wienzeile apartments' flat façade with windows almost flush with the walls revealed experimentation with new materials and simplification of design.[33] For Wagner the theorist this was the embodiment of the prevailing modern style and individual.

However, by the time that Leonie von Puttkamer was living in one of the buildings, Wagner's duality of commerce and domicile and the rational style he had developed for the commercial section of the Wienzeile buildings took precedence. "It was as if modern man's 'businesslike essence' (Wagner's phrase) and the style appropriate to his work life came to dominate all dimensions of his existence."[34] This change resulted from the bureaucratization of government and business a few years after the buildings were erected in 1888–1889. The expansion of a centralized administration meant that more space was required beyond one or two lower floors of apartment buildings. Thereafter, in the apartment buildings that Wagner built, his breakthrough with utilitarian forms reached its fulfilment in the triumph of the office over the home, and the adventitious ornament disappeared in the face of more restrained lines and patterns and the uniform cellular space of a commercial building. For example, the upper stories of Wagner's Neustiftgasse 40 constructed between 1909–1910 were in the style of the business section, unlike the Wienzeile buildings where the upper residential quarters were independent in form and decoration from the commercial sections below.[35]

From 1910, Wagner turned away from the primacy of the aesthetic towards emphasizing the functional and the technical. He further synthesized new technology and new art, and valued massive uniformity, believing that most modern men would rather live in a metropolis than in the country and that therefore the city must adapt to new modern needs. He affirmed the pedestrian urban experience of the man of business or the shopper, and he glorified the commercial stores that he saw as part of the infinitely expandable city. While critics like the romantic archaist Sitte stressed the artisanal tradition and embraced Ringstrasse historicism, Wagner, the rational functionalist, embraced the dynamism of the street and a bourgeois affirmation of modern technology. Sitte was fearful of the changes time wrought and tried to envision a city of constrained space around the human and socializing confines of the square. But Wagner, even more so than the Ringstrasse liberals before him, sought to move with the times, keep the street and men in motion, and give them clear direction. Style for Wagner was there to reinforce the power of the street, movement, and modernity.[36]

How do we understand what life was like in the Wienzeile buildings, and what were the attendant cultural implications for our analysis of the story of Csonka and her lover?

On the one hand, representing a departure from old world roles, this new secessionist building matched the modern, urban, libertine lifestyle Leonie von Puttkamer had carved out for herself, out of choice and financial need, as well as her break from an aristocratic past and her self-renewal in a modern life of her own making. The new modern architecture built to match the social dynamics of Wagner's time seemed fit for a New Woman like her. Matching her colorful life, Leonie lived in a building lavishly decorated with brightly colored tiles, sculpture, and wrought iron that Wagner pioneered. On the other hand, we can reverse the direction of this analysis and see how increasing freedom for women, as well as Leonie's economic difficulties, allowed her to seize on a different meaning for the Wienzeile buildings than Wagner's vision of them as befitting rational men of business. Her "business" was to live as a high-class prostitute; she was able to conduct her business at home and, paradoxically and unexpectedly perhaps, in line with Wagner's original concept, blur the boundaries between work and home. Moreover, Wagner used Klimt's secessionist style but avoided his emphasis on the erotic and the instinctual in favor of efficiency and rationality—as with the glass bathtub that for Wagner emphasized transparency and purity. But Leonie von Puttkamer's excessive lifestyle and extravagant outfits brought these elements to the fore; she herself could be said to reflect the secessionist vision generally and the erotic in particular.[37] The very location of the buildings in an area that had been renewed and reconstructed in modern ways provided her with the opportunity to define her life anew in the city. The flamboyant baroness lived in a ménage à trois with Ernst Waldmann, a dealer in wholesale cooking oil, as his mistress, and with his wife Karla as her lover (first spotted at Semmering by Gretl). The married couple provided Leonie with financial security.[38]

The importance of the city in influencing and enabling Gretl and Leonie's meetings is revealed in various ways, not only in architecture but also in transport. Gretl told her biographers that after learning that Leonie lived in the Linke Wienzeile, she remembers frequently getting off the tram at the Kettenbrückengasse stop.[39] Indeed, it was one of the Stadtbahn stations and it stood right in front of the Wienzeile residence. The Stadtbahn was also designed by Otto Wagner in the secessionist style, structurally completed in 1896, and opened in 1899. The Kettenbrückengasse stop is also near the Naschmarkt, the city's largest outdoor food market. Whenever Gretl had free time, she would wait for Leonie in the comfort of a new, modern phone booth near Leonie's house, without attracting unwanted attention. Even in

Figure 3 The Linke Wienzeile building, Majolica House, by Otto Wagner
Source: Wikimedia.[40]

Figure 4 The Linke Wienzeile building, Medallion House, by Otto Wagner
Source: Wikimedia.[41]

the age of consumption, with flourishing stores that turned women into consumers and made window-shopping and strolling alone a respectable activity, a woman walking alone in the street, unaccompanied by a man, could still be identified with prostitution.[42]

Gretl finished high school but, with her upper-middle-class background, she did not seek a job as did an increasing number of other middle-class women. Thus, she had time to pursue the baroness while using various tricks and taking advantage of the city's new sites that enabled her to escape from home for a few hours without supervision. Her father spent all his time in his city office, concerned with the war. He was busy with his Galician oil and solid paraffin companies, helping in the military effort, and worried about reversals at the Russian front, which left him no time for his daughter. Gretl's mother took no interest in her and her older brother who used to watch over her was still at the front. These circumstances of class, gender, family, and the war left Gretl freer than usual to roam the city. Eventually, she was brave enough to speak to the baroness, saying: "I am only here for one reason: to see you."[43]

Figure 5 Café Dobner (on Linke Wienzeile) with Thonet chairs, c.1900
Source: Wien Museum Online Sammlung [Vienna Museum Online Collection].[44]

Thereafter, Gretl waited openly for her beloved in front of the Secession Building (Secessionsgebäude), the famous construction by Joseph Maria Olbrich, one of Wagner's younger students. Olbrich designed the Secession Building as a modernized temple, hinting that the function of art was a form of religion for Vienna's secular elite.[45] It represented the cultural revolution of the Vienna Secession, though in the last year of the war it was transformed into a field hospital and, as she waited for Leonie, Gretl was exposed to wounded or badly disabled soldiers—a sight common in other European cities too.[46] Gretl would accompany the baroness home, stopping at Café Dobner, a popular meeting place for artists founded in 1795.[47] At this time, the café was furnished with modern bentwood chairs, designed a hundred years earlier by Michael Thonet, which by the twentieth century were popular, iconic, and mass produced.[48] Gretl, who had never frequented a café before, enjoyed the forbidden freedom of being a

Figure 6 Interior views of Café Dobner. The photos show the café's new design by the architect Carl Stephann, following the renovation that began in March 1907
Source: *Das Interieur: Wiener Monatshefte für angeandte Kunst*, Tafel 57 (Anton Schroll & Co., 1908), 105.

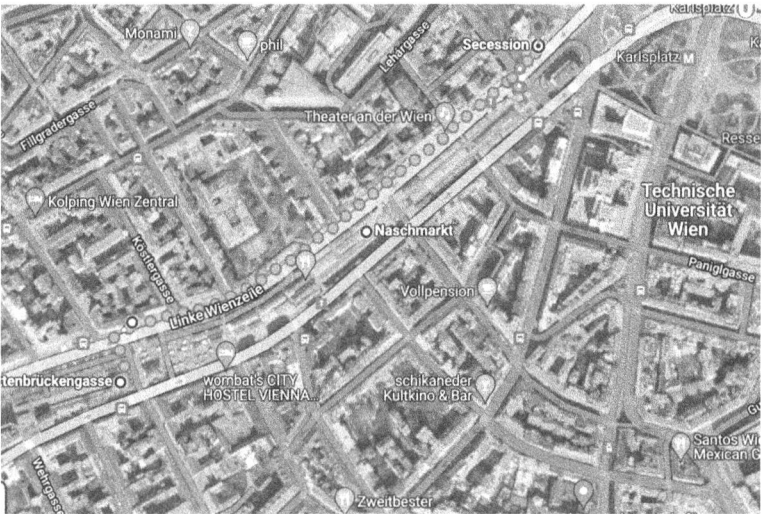

Figure 7 Map showing the landmarks, marked by white dots, in central Vienna where Leonie and Gretl walked
Source: Google Maps.

young woman in a modern coffeehouse, one of Vienna's great urban cultural institutions that had traditionally been the domain of men but was now also used by women. She also enjoyed the new privilege of strolling with her beloved through the streets and the Naschmarkt.[49]

Unfortunately for Gretl, her father's office was located close by, on Linke Wienzeile between the Secessionsgebäude and Kettenbrückengasse. Indeed, the whole affair took place in a small, modernized radius of a ten-minute walk, as the map shows.

Csonka's Action, Csonka vs Freud, and the Baroness's Story

Csonka's father had heard gossip about his daughter associating with Puttkamer, who was known both as a beauty and a high-class courtesan and homosexual. As we already know from Freud's account, once when strolling with Leonie, Gretl saw her father crossing the street. In her biography Gretl said she was sure he had seen her and so she ran away. However, when she stopped to look back, she was surprised to see her father boarding a tram seeming not to have noticed her at all (in contrast to Freud's description of his angry glance). Filled with shame and embarrassment, she tried to explain why she had fled to Baroness Puttkamer who coldly and sarcastically retorted: "Under the circumstances, ma chère, it would be best, if in the future you would spare me your half-hearted demonstrations of love. They just spoil my mood."[50] Nearing the station at Kettenbrückengasse, and distraught that her beloved no longer wanted her, Gretl attempted suicide by jumping onto the tracks. However, she survived and upon her recovery, the meetings with Leonie resumed.

Thus, while in Freud's account the suicide attempt at the station was anchored in the familial Oedipal drama, for Gretl it was rooted in romantic love and served as (a possibly Wertherian cultural) declaration of despair stemming from true same-sex love. These differences are key to the juxtaposition that can be made between Freud's and Csonka's framing of the narrative. A modern train station was both the background and the catalyst for Gretl's sudden ad hoc decision to commit suicide. But this location was the focus of an important psychoanalytic point which reveals where Freud and Csonka's narratives perhaps differ most. After discussing this further, I will show how active Csonka was more broadly, both in her actions towards Freud and with her beloved.

For Freud, Csonka's actions at the train station stemmed directly from her Oedipus complex, and were triggered by the father's "angry glance" when he saw his daughter in the company of her lady.[51] The father's reaction was significant for Freud because of his interpretation of Gretl's same-sex love stemming from her Oedipal complex and family relations. He understood that this made her chose a homosexual love-object as she struggled to (a) substitute her mother with the lady-love; (b) see her lady as a reminder of her older brother; (c) express her psychological disappointment of her father (and men) due to the birth of a younger brother; and (d) repudiate her love of men and the feminine role that would also include giving birth. Furthermore, as we saw, this led Freud to claim that this female homosexual had, in effect, "changed into a man" (in her behavior and attitude); that is, she took her mother instead of her father as her love-object and behaved like a male lover towards her beloved lady. What mattered to Freud was that in her behavior towards her love-object she assumed the masculine role.[52]

In Freud's text, the girl explained her suicide attempt as stemming from the fact that after she had confessed to her beloved that the man who had cast the angry glance was her father (who had forbidden their friendship), "the lady became incensed at this and ordered the girl to leave her then and there, and never again to wait for her or to address her—the affair must now come to an end." Then, "in her despair at having thus lost her loved one for ever, she wanted to put an end to herself."[53] However, Freud argued that the analysis and her dreams disclosed "a deeper interpretation," according to which the attempted suicide was determined by two more motives—the fulfilment of a punishment (self-punishment) and the fulfilment of a wish concerning her family romance. Freud explained:

> As the latter it meant the attainment of the very wish which, when frustrated, had driven her into homosexuality—namely, the wish to have a child by her father, for now she "fell" through her father's fault.[54] The fact that at that moment the lady had spoken in just the same terms as her father, and had uttered the same prohibition, forms the connecting link between this deep interpretation and the superficial one of which the girl herself was conscious. From the point of view of self-punishment the girl's action shows us that she had developed in her unconscious strong death-wishes against one or other of her parents—perhaps against her father, out of revenge for impeding her love, but more probably against her mother too, when she was pregnant with the little brother.[55]

As Freud continues with his theory in the sessions, Csonka seems to withdraw from him or, in Freud's eyes, to show resistance to analysis. In response to one of his explanations, "she replied in an inimitable tone, 'How very interesting,' as though she were a grande dame being taken over a museum and glancing through her lorgnon at objects to which she was completely indifferent."[56] This almost comic description meant for Freud that she was hiding behind a protective barrier that allowed her to maintain her stance, as if to say, as Freud put it: "'It would be all very fine,' thinks the patient, often quite consciously, 'if I were obliged to believe what the man says, but there is no question of that, and so long as this is so I need change nothing.'"[57] This barrier and the limited positive transference to her analyst led Freud to terminate the analysis.

There is more to say on this point and the active role that Gretl Csonka played in the analytic treatment. Historians Birgit Lang and Katie Sutton argue that in contrast to the direct and descriptive approach of the sexologists in their case histories that often included the patient's first-person narration, psychoanalysis "presented a new discursive model, which channeled and constrained the patients' 'voices', reducing their agency and apparent authority, in order to problematize and question what they said."[58]

It is true that in Freud's writing of the case, we hear the patient's voice through Freud's words as he controlled the narrative writing. However, it might be helpful to give more weight to the fact that, even more than in the meetings with the sexologists that were at times undertaken without their patients' consent, in the psychoanalytic session and in the analyst-patient dynamics, the patient's active (even eager and dedicated) collaboration is required in the disclosure of his or her biography, fantasies, associations, and dreams. The patient's positive or negative reactions to interpretations from the analyst and the transference towards the analyst are key, whereas in encounters with the sexologist they are not. In other words, the psychoanalytic patient *by definition* cannot be entirely passive. This is a fine example of the analytic dynamic, as once Gretl actively and mockingly refused to engage in a real dialogue with Freud, he had no alternative but to end the therapy.

Furthermore, in contrast to Freud, in the biography it is clear that Csonka saw herself as driven more by romantic love for Puttkamer and less by her internal family relations. Although she was concerned that her father would cause a row, she was more distraught that her lady wanted nothing more to do with her. She said: "Leonie, please, I want to be with you, always, I want to be at your side day and night, and everyone will know that, but..." Whereupon Leonie responded, "This 'but' is precisely the reason why it is better that we are not seen together in the future. Run along and goodbye."[59] As Puttkamer was walking away, Csonka was crying and wondered whether Leonie realized that she was the sole focus of her emotions and that keeping their connection alive was essential to Csonka's survival. Although Csonka was worried that her father would punish her, she was more worried about how to continue her life if her beloved no longer wanted her. Without hesitating, she then decided to try to kill herself.[60]

Additionally, it seems that Csonka was actively utilizing and reworking a chivalrous or romantic script that was culturally available to her to express desire towards another woman. Adopting the role of actively seeking the attention of another woman, she imitated the attributes of a desperate lover who, in her society, would usually be a heterosexual male. Nonetheless, this did not mean to her that she had "changed into a man" as Freud would have it in his medical model of psychological inversion. Rather, this simply enabled her to express her desire in the terms of available cultural symbols and expected patterns of behavior. This choice can indeed be seen as a "queer" one (in both senses of the word), as culturally women in love usually expressed their feelings differently and in less actively seeking ways. But to

Csonka this did not suggest she had changed into a man—either in her words or in her dress and appearance. Behaving in a manner coded as male did not mean she identified as male, nor did it mean she had "become a man." Rather, she drew upon rich cultural codes of conduct to act on her erotic feelings (as well as a degree of homosexual self-hatred) as she navigated the less charted and codified territory of female same-sex desire.[61]

As the war finally ended, in the summer of 1918, the Csonka family returned from the summer vacation to the altered, postwar city. Herr Csonka was busy rescuing his business, which was tied to the collapsed Austro-Hungarian empire, moving parts of it to France and the Netherlands. The baroness had left the Waldmanns for the much wealthier Count Apponyi, and was living near a tram stop in Ungargasse where the Csonka family lived too.[62]

Gretl was invited to Leonie's apartment and, again, following conventions of heterosexual romantic love, she brought her flowers and poems. In return, Leonie taught her about sexuality, introducing the innocent Gretl to the then-popular erotic novel *Memoirs of Josephine Mutzenbacher*. This book was first published anonymously in Vienna in 1906; it was written by Felix Salten, the famous Jewish writer of *Bambi, a Life in the Woods* (1923), and friend of Arthur Schnitzler and other members of the Young Vienna (Jung Wien) movement who challenged Victorian morality and promoted psychological and sexual openness.[63] The novel's descriptions of sexual activity brought home to the inexperienced Gretl the nature of her beloved's affairs with both men and women.[64]

It is interesting to learn a little of Leonie's family background as it gives some insights into who she was and the lifestyle she was able to create for herself in the newly modernized Vienna. Bertha Hermine Leonie von Puttkamer, Leonie's full name, was born on January 10, 1891, in Schloss Henkenhagen, Kreis Regenwalde.[65] Both her parents were from noble Prussian families. Her mother, Anna Louise née von Alvensleben (1965–1945),[66] was born in Düsseldorf, the daughter of Count (or Graf, in German) Friedrich Werner (1838–1912)[67] and Hermine von Alvensleben née von Nagell (1846–1901).[68] On September 17, 1885,[69] Anna Louise married the Kammerjunker Günther Georg Peter von Puttkamer of Schlackow,[70] with whom she gave birth to Leonie and her two older siblings, Juliana Anna Erike (1886)[71] and Agathon Robert Werner (1889).[72] In 1903, Leonie's parents divorced after her father learned that his wife was having affairs with both men and women.[73] On October 6 in the same year, Günther married Dorothea "Doly" Planck von Planckburg (1877–1954), daughter of Karl

Franz and Bohumilia Maria Planck von Planckburg née Krüzner.[74] According to Rieder and Voigt, Leonie was not fond of her step-mother at all. In 1911, during Leonie's visit to her father, Doly had Leonie examined by a Berlin specialist because she was thought to be "mentally disturbed." The specialist determined that Leonie was sexually abnormal.[75]

One year later, on October 8, 1904, Anna Louise married again, to Count Ludwig Karl von Holnstein, Hereditary Imperial Councillor of the Crown of Bavaria (Erblicher Reichsrat der Krone Bayrens) (from September 21, 1868, in Munich, until October 11, 1930). The Count's first marriage had been dissolved in 1903. The couple resided at the Holnstein family estate, Schloss Thalhausen, Freising, Upper Bavaria.[76]

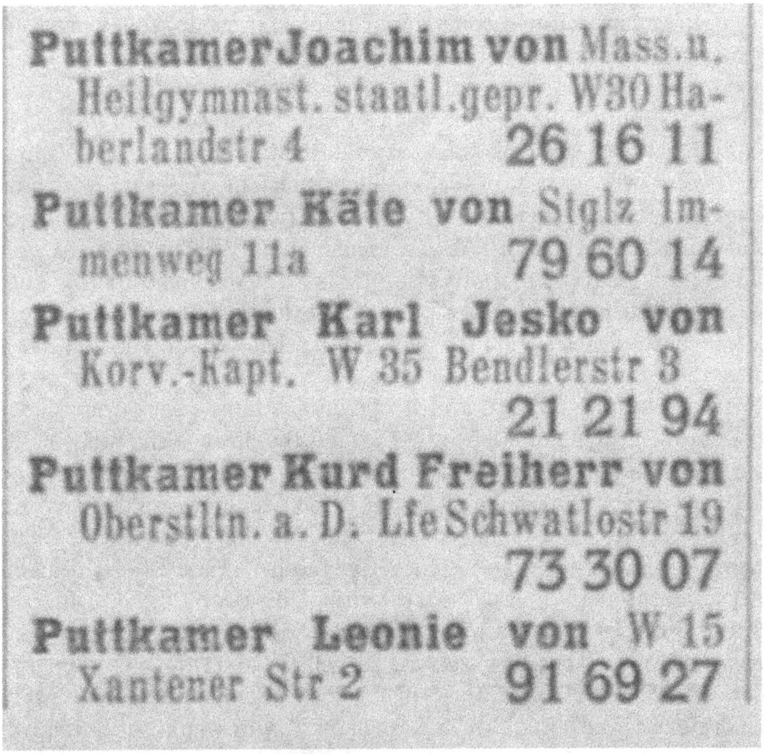

Puttkamer Joachim von Mass. u. Heilgymnast. staatl. gepr. W 30 Haberlandstr 4   **26 16 11**

Puttkamer Käte von Stglz Immenweg 11a   **79 60 14**

Puttkamer Karl Jesko von Korv.-Kapt. W 35 Bendlerstr 3   **21 21 94**

Puttkamer Kurd Freiherr von Oberstltn. a. D. Lfe Schwatlostr 19   **73 30 07**

Puttkamer Leonie von W 15 Xantener Str 2   **91 69 27**

Figure 8 Extract from the Amtliches Fernsprechbuch für den Bezirk der Reichspostdirektion Berlin, (Official telephone book for the district of the Reichspostdirektion Berlin), 1938
Source: www.genealoglyindexer.org.

Anna Gräfin von Holnstein aus Bayern, geb. von Alvensleben mit
ihren berühmten Zwerg-Cocker-Spaniels.

Figure 9 Leonie's mother, Countess Anna Louise von Holnstein née von Alvensleben
Source: www.ancestry.com.

Figure 10 Leonie's father, Count Günther von Puttkamer
Source: *Wiener Salonblatt*, September 21, 1907, 7.

Figure 11 Leonie's mother-in-law, Dorothea "Doly" Planck von Planckburg
Source: Wiener Salonblatt, September 21, 1907, 5.

Figure 12 Schlackow Castle in Pomerania, Leonie's childhood home
Source: *Wiener Salonblatt,* September 21, 1907, 11.[77]

Leonie came to Vienna in 1917 from Munich. Following her parents' divorce, her mother was no longer accepted at court and her father lost the family fortune—to the agriculture crisis in Prussia at the end of the nineteenth century, and finally to rampant inflation following the First World War. Thus, Leonie lost her inheritance and had to find work. Her family background gave her access to aristocratic circles and as a young adult she began having affairs in Vienna with men and women for financial security.[78]

Leonie and Gretl's intimate meetings were again under threat when, with the end of the war and the consolidation of the new republic, Gretl's brother returned home, and her father focused his attention on his daughter as his wife had reported on the frequent visits to the baroness. They decided to send Gretl to Professor Freud to restore her to normality.[79] Therefore, for four months, every afternoon, Gretl travelled alone on modern public transport to see Freud. Leaving her parents' flat in Neulinggasse, she took the O tram to Rennweg, transferred to the 71 heading to Schwarzenbergplatz, transferred again to the tram that circled the Ring, and disembarked at Schottentor. She then walked to Freud's house and clinic at Berggasse 19 on the other side of town at the opposite end of the Ringstrasse (see Figure 13).[80]

Thus, while a train station was where Gretl tried to kill herself, the modern train system that was built in Vienna also connected the two women to one another, and one of them to Freud, allowing not only movement across space, but also partial liberation from family ties,

Figure 13 Map of Vienna showing Csonka's trip to Freud's clinic
Source: Google Maps.

anonymity, and an intensification of emotional life. It helped to create the conditions for meetings between the protagonists of this same-sex love, and offered one of them a route to Freud's house and to an analysis of her life, both psychologically and historically.[81]

Seeing Freud and Assimilated Jewish Life in Vienna

Gretl was reluctant about attending sessions with Freud five times a week. She had heard rumors that he dealt with "crazy people and can heal souls." When she mentioned him to family friends, they responded with an embarrassed silence or a contemptuous glance. Gretl told her biographers that her father saw her suicide attempt as a final sign that Puttkamer's influence would destroy her reputation; he warned his daughter that given the high cost of the sessions, he expected cooperation and a successful outcome.[82] Despite her reservations, Gretl realized that she loved him and wanted his approval, so she accepted the penance.[83] This, we should note, contrasts with Freud's assessment that in her relationship with her father she mainly wanted revenge.

On her first visit to Freud, Gretl reported that she was so nervous that she made a curtesy and was about to kiss Freud's hand, before he rebuffed her, in a somewhat cavalier gesture of gender reversal as if she were a man (at least in Freud's reading) paying court to a woman (Freud in this case). This, she thought, was the first and last time he chuckled as otherwise she found him "earnest and totally unapproachable though not unsympathetic."[84] In general, she found him "uninteresting; an old man with a lovely white beard who poses sticky questions and makes unbelievable assertions." She could not decide if the analysis was "more boring or more obnoxious."[85] She viewed the stiff Persian rug on Freud's couch to be "a most unsuitable covering."[86] Freud was seated behind her and asked questions or said "Ja" in a quiet monotone as she lay on the couch. It felt as if he were "breathing down my neck," she thought.[87]

Freud instructed her to tell him everything that came to mind and asked her to write down her dreams. Gretl found this difficult as she felt nothing happened to her and she could not remember her dreams. During the sessions, therefore, she kept quiet until the silence became burdensome and she felt both anxious and terribly bored. Freud then broke the spell and returned to asking her questions about her family. Initially, she had no idea where these sessions were leading, but she did eventually note that she had begun to observe her parents and brothers more closely, and that events from the past which had seemed insignificant began to preoccupy her.[88]

It was also Freud's questioning that led Gretl to ask her mother about the family's Jewish past and to reveal it in full.[89] Her mother told of the transition of her Jewish family from Galicia to Vienna and its rise to a higher class. Thus, we also learn the crucial historical fact that the meetings between Professor Freud and Margarethe Csonka were encounters between an assimilated and secular Jewish man and an assimilated Jewish (yet baptized) female homosexual in a context that loaded these labels with complex meanings.

It is worth delving more deeply into Gretl's background to understand her own family history within the context of the changing city of

Vienna, the new paths opening up to its inhabitants, and the rising antisemitism.

Margarethe Csonka was born in Lemberg on April 26, 1900[90] to Jewish parents, Arpad and Irma Csonka née Kern. Irma was born in Vienna on February 19, 1876,[91] the youngest daughter of Rebeka "Rika"[92] Kern née Berger (who died when Irma was only eleven, on January 8, 1887, at the age of 39),[93] and of Emanuel "Mano" Kern (1835–1891), a civil servant with the railway.[94] Her parents married in Szeged, Hungary, on January 13, 1869.[95] Irma had three older siblings, Hugo (b. 1870),[96] Viktor (1872–1916),[97] and Josephine (b. 1873).[98] After her father's death, Irma was sent to live with relatives in Lemberg.[99] Like Irma, Arpad Csonka, born on October 2, 1869 as Moricz Abraham Moshe Csonka,[100] came from a poor, religious, Jewish family in Budapest where his father Ignacz (born in 1839 in Buda, and died in 1899 in Budapest), son of Joseph Csonka and Judit née Klein,[101] was the impoverished owner of a clothing shop.[102] Arpad was the second of four children—Sandor (Shimshon) Csonka (b. 1867),[103] Aranka (Yitel) Csonka (1877–1953),[104] and Malvine (Matel) Csonka (b. 1871) who died in infancy two years after her birth.[105] Upon graduating from commercial college, Arpad joined the petroleum branch of the Rothschild consortium's oil refinery in 1886[106] in order to support his family. As a Jewish man eager to assimilate and succeed in an antisemitic society, he moved to Lemberg, then the capital of Galicia, where access to the promising oil and paraffin industry was easier than in other cities of the Austro-Hungarian empire.[107] In Lemberg, Arpad married Irma on October 31, 1897;[108] she gave birth to a son, Hans, in 1899, and to Gretl in 1900. In 1902, Arpad founded the Boryslaw Crude Oil Transport and Storage Company outside Lemberg and made a great fortune. He employed local unskilled laborers as well as chemical engineers and other professionals, many of whom were Jewish.[109]

Living in an antisemitic society, Arpad, like others of his generation, grew alienated from his parents' Jewish community in Budapest. Out of love for his religious mother, Bertha "Betty" née Schulhof (1848–1923),[110] he went to synagogue on the high holidays and promised her not to be baptized. Arpad was, however, determined that his children would not be marked as poor Eastern European Jews which, in the eyes of antisemites of the time, signified disease and degeneracy. When he married Irma, he suggested that their future offspring should be baptized as Catholic. She agreed and in return asked to return to her native city to continue advancing his work and social standing there—again, a common move among Jews at the time who transferred to Vienna in their thousands following the emancipation of Jews.[111] In Vienna, Irma gave birth to Gretl's younger brother, Paul August Csonka (1905),[112] and to Alexander Walter[113] when Gretl was seventeen.

These facts of modern Jewish life are important to fully understand the 1920 case. In the sessions with Freud, Gretl argued that the Csonkas had improved their position and reassured themselves that "everything is going to be just fine."[114] Yet Freud, himself an assimilated "Godless Jew" with a complex attitude towards his Judaism, though he never denied it,[115] remarked that she had told him of her baptism on three occasions and was perhaps revealing the family anxiety or arrogance about this newly acquired status. Indeed, when socializing among Arpad's business contacts, Irma felt nervous, inexperienced, and not sophisticated enough. Despite their relatively high financial standing, they lacked the connections and the easy feeling of being "at home" that Christian families enjoyed in the city. This may be a better and more historical way of understanding Irma's tension than relying solely on the label "neurotic" assigned to her by Freud.[116]

Indeed, like Irma and Arpad, other less fortunate Jews moved to Vienna, especially from the eastern part of the kingdom where they faced violent antisemitism. At the turn of the century, when Jews comprised 10 percent of the population of Vienna, antisemitism also grew, especially under the mayorship of Karl Lueger. Some viewed Irma and Arpad's financial success as a threat to Christian Vienna and therefore the family did not talk about their Jewish heritage. Gretl did not like to consider herself Jewish (a view she maintained most of her life[117]). The family did well after moving to Vienna in 1902: they rented a nine-room flat on Neulinggasse in 1909, in Landstrasse one of the centers of Vienna's Jewish life, and were able to keep a cook, two maids, a governess, and a nanny—even during the war. Nonetheless, if the children made too much noise their father would complain that it was "as loud as a Jewish *schul*," which Gretl viewed according to the antisemitic terms that surrounded her as a terrible thing.[118]

Gretl told Freud that it was her mother who made decisions in the household. She sympathized with her father for putting up with her mother, yet she also admired her subtlety, entitlement, and inconsistent tyranny. Gretl described her mother as "often terribly nervous and dissatisfied and full of the most absurd fears—of thieves, fires, and flood. There is nothing that she doesn't think is dangerous."[119] Seeing every woman, including her own daughter, as a competitor, Irma told a man in Semmering that Gretl was the child of an acquaintance to make herself appear younger and divert his interest away from her

Figure 14 Irma Csonka, 1915
Source: Sigmund-Freud-Privatstiftung.

Figure 15 Arpad Csonka, 1915
Source: Sigmund-Freud-Privatstiftung.

daughter. Gretl viewed her mother's flirtations as a disgrace to her father whom she saw as a kind man she respected and loved and did not want to hurt.[120] Freud suggested to Gretl that her mother's jealous, harsh attitude made her search for a mother-substitute to whom she could become passionately attached; he offered Gretl his suspicion of her idealization of her father. Yet Gretl's narrative seems to reveal a more genuine side to her attitude towards her father.

Following the session in which Freud spoke of this suspicion, in breach of her promises, Gretl went directly to meet Leonie at Café Herrenhof on Herrengasse 10, which during the interwar period was well known among the city's literati. It attracted artists, young writers, and intellectuals and thus, importantly, she was unlikely to meet her father there. The café's interior was designed by the Jewish architect Stefan Fayans, a sought-after designer of the new cinemas and restaurants that were being built in the city, who created new public spaces in which men and women, Christians and Jews, could socialize. Again, we see how this modern urban setting, with its art nouveau style, was conducive to Gretl meeting Leonie regularly without attracting attention.[121]

It seems that different types of religiously charged identifications affected Csonka's own identification with the Christian Puttkamer during these meetings and as she fell in love with her. This would make her freer socially and less susceptible to the racist discrimination among the upper class, even if she lost her respectable status and became more sexually emancipated and a libertine New Woman, like the aristocratic baroness. Although Puttkamer was involved in a transactional sexual relationship, Gretl Csonka could borrow from the Christian discourse on prostitution that positioned her as a savior of her coquettish lover. Thus, these two women's sexual roles, identifications, and desires can be situationally positioned.[122]

These meetings between the two women obviously made a mockery of Freud's treatment and revealed that Gretl actively used the time frame of analysis for her own interests and needs, as she felt unable to cope without Leonie who, she believed, was the only person who truly understood her. Thus, in its way, the analysis allowed for the continuation of the same-sex meetings. Gretl told herself that the meetings in coffee houses were innocent, as if she were telling Freud and her father that she herself was innocent in regard to the baroness. The meeting immediately after the session described above with Freud— who knew nothing of it happening—was ideal as nobody noticed she was late home, and the café provided a safe place for the women to meet. Gretl angrily told Leonie that she found Freud offensive·

Figure 16 Café Herrenhof
Source: Geschichtewiki.[123]

Just imagine! For some time now he has been asking me in great detail about my parents and my brothers ... And do you know what he told me today? That I would have liked to have a child with my father, and because my mother had the child, I hate her and my father as well, and *that's* why I turn away from men altogether. It is completely outrageous![124]

In response, Leonie teased her, saying that she was indeed perverted, a label which brought Gretl close to tears. Enraged, she continued: "He is such a creep. A disgusting brute. He has the dirtiest fantasies a human being can have ... By now he ought to realize that I'm as innocent as a five-year-old."[125] Thereafter, Gretl had to force herself to continue seeing him. She wished that Freud would tell her father she was innocent so she could cease attending the sessions. She became increasingly reluctant during the sessions, diverting attention away from her relationship with Leonie by recounting one anecdote after another. As she ran out of things to say and did not remember her dreams, she wondered whether he suspected that she was meeting Leonie regularly. To overcome this fear, she presented these meetings as dreams. In his writing, Freud indeed recounted how her dreams (which he interpreted as heterosexual wishes to marry rather than about Leonie) seemed false to him. But it did not occur to him that she lied intentionally.[126]

Coincidently, and unfortunately for Gretl, Leonie had her hair done twice a week at Salon Geppert,[127] the same place as Csonka's mother. The hairdresser told her mother that Gretl was seeing the baroness, and her mother told Gretl that in the future she should take care as "Papa and Freud won't be pleased to hear about it."[128] Unable to trust her mother not to tell Freud, Gretl decided to tell him the "dreamed" half-truth facts about her meetings, not knowing whether he believed her or not, in the short period left before the summer vacation in July. In the first session following the summer holidays, Freud told Gretl of his decision to conclude the analysis, which she accepted with relief. She felt that she was well-intentioned and had done everything required of her, and she hoped Freud would reassure her father that Leonie had not led her into her bed so he would leave her in peace, as "not everything can be changed." When they were separating, Gretl reported to her biographers with pride, Freud told her, "You have such shrewd eyes. I would not want to have you as my enemy."[129]

Throughout her life, Margarethe Csonka considered Freud to be "a fool who had a filthy imagination."[130] Yet we saw that the analysis did give her a new way of learning about and looking at her family's past and Jewish background. Though she disliked and rejected his theoretical explanations (that befitted in part his heterosexual, phallocentric Oedipal model), he did not respond with a derogatory or strictly negative attitude towards her love of Baroness Leonie von Puttkamer. He seemed to accept her love as genuine and her homosexuality as a deviation from heterosexuality rather than a perversion in the sense common among other medical men. As a Jewish male doctor, he was willing to accept her as an assimilated Jewish female homosexual who was socially different (both as a Jew, even when she denied this background, and a homosexual), but not ill.[131] Thus, despite the unsuccessful analysis, and the fact that Gretl did not feel good about her sessions with Freud, she did not get a negative reaction from him, and in retrospect described him as "not unsympathetic."

Notes

1 Ines Rieder and Diana Voigt, eds., *The Story of Sidonie C.: Freud's Famous "Case of Female Homosexuality,"* trans. Jill Hannum and Ines Rieder (Budapest: Helena History Press, 2019), xii. It was first published in German in 2000.

2 Her estate was deposited in the Freud Museum in Vienna under the name Margarethe Csonka-Trautenegg.

3 Despite its many fantastic achievements, the biography (which I am grateful to partly rely on here) poses problems for professional historians as its authors chose to write it in the format of a memoir. As this is not an autobiography, Csonka is not the sole author of the publication: her biographers chose to narrate her words and what happened to her in a voice that combines interviews with her narration of events and lots of hindsight. Thus, it is hard for historians to point to the different layers of reliability while using the biography. (Where possible, I have indicated what are direct quotations and what is paraphrased.) Nonetheless, it can still serve the purpose of crafting an alternative narrative from the patient's point of view. We should also remember that Freud's writing, too, can be seen as a fictional narrative, as Fuss claimed. See Diana Fuss, "Fallen Woman: The Psychogenesis of a Case of Homosexuality in a Woman," in *That Obscure Subject of Desire: Freud's Female Homosexual Revisited*, eds. Ronnie C. Lesser and Erica Schoenberg (New York: Routledge, 1999), 54–75. Csonka's testimony to her biographers was given years after her meeting with Freud, a fact that no doubt influenced the way she chose to present it. Nonetheless, on an epistemological level, despite this gap in time, we can see how both offer different yet complementary narratives, each conducted with opposing interests in mind.

4 See also Michal Shapira, "Indecently Exposed: The Male Body and Vagrancy in Metropolitan London before the Fin de Siècle," *Gender & History* 30, no. 1 (March 2018): 52–69.

5 Views of the Panhans Hotel can be found at https://grand-hotel-panhans-semmering.booked.net/.

6 Rieder and Voigt, *The Story of Sidonie C.*, 8.
7 The photograph was published in *Wiener Salonblatt* on December 24, 1921, 6. The original caption read "Baronesse Leonie von Puttkamer, Atelier Helene Zimmeraur, Gumpendorfer St. 32, Vienna VI." *Wiener Salonblatt* was a weekly journal (fortnightly since 1919), published in Vienna from 1870 to 1938. Its "pages were filled with news of the court and the aristocracy—accounts of the parties, the engagements, the marriages, the hunts, the dances of the eighty families who, according to Napoleon, ruled Austria," as explained in Max Graf, *Composer and Critic: Two Hundred Years of Musical Criticism* (New York: Norton & Company, 1946), 275. Photographs of male or female aristocrats were included, with or without corresponding text about the person portrayed. No text accompanied Leonie's photo. Today the newspaper is mainly known among scholars for publishing Hugo Wolf's (1860–1903) musical criticisms.
8 Ibid., 9. August Sarnitz, *Otto Wagner* (New York: Taschen, 2018), 47–50.
9 My analysis of the architectural changes is based directly on Carl E. Schorske, *Fin-de-siècle Vienna* (New York: Vintage, 1980), chap. 2, 24–116. See also Elana Shapira, *Style and Seduction: Jewish Patrons, Architecture, and Design in Fin de Siècle Vienna* (Waltham, MA: Brandeis University Press, 2016). Specifically, Elana Shapira shows in great detail the cultural relevance of building, interiors, and design objects to Jews in Vienna as she follows the contributions of Jewish patrons, businessmen, journalists, and authors to the remaking of the city. Modernizing the city held specific meaning for acculturated and assimilated Jews, especially when the illusion of security was breaking down with the rise of antisemitism. She shows the critical Jewish influence on Viennese modernism. She also argues that new styles, aesthetics, good taste, and appropriate dress were dear to those who tried to stabilize their identity and find a new place for themselves, transforming "Jewishness" from crime to legitimacy amid hostility. This argument is relevant to other minorities as well, such as women and homosexuals. See the images of the Csonka's family's elaborate dress. See also Anthony Alofsin, *When Buildings Speak: Architecture as Language in the Habsburg Empire and Its Aftermath, 1867–1933* (Chicago: Chicago University Press, 2006); Frederic Bedoire, *The Jewish Contribution to Modern Architecture, 1830–1930* (Jersey City, NJ: Ktav Publishing House, 2004); Steven Beller, "'The Jew Belongs in the Coffeehouse': Jews, Central Europe and Modernity," in *The Viennese Café and Fin-de-Siècle Culture*, eds. Charlotte Ashby, Tag Gronberg, and Simon Shaw-Miller (New York: Berghahn, 2013), 50–48; Steven Beller, *Vienna and the Jews, 1867–1938: A Cultural History* (Cambridge: Cambridge, 1989); Tag Gronberg, *Vienna: City of Modernity, 1890–1914* (Oxford: Peter Lang, 2007); Marsha L. Rozenblit, *The Jews of Vienna, 1867–1914: Assimilation and Identity* (Albany: State University of New York Press, 1983); Alison Rose, *Jewish Women in Fin de Siècle Vienna* (Austin: University of Texas Press, 2008); Leslie Topp, *Architecture and Truth in Fin-de-Siècle Vienna* (Cambridge: Cambridge University Press, 2004); Daniel M. Vyleta, *Crime, Jews and News: Vienna 1895–1914* (New York: Berghahn, 2007).
10 Schorske, *Fin-de-siècle Vienna*, 24–62.

11   Ibid., 62.
12   Ibid., 62–72.
13   Quoted in Sarnitz, *Otto Wagner*, 7.
14   Schorske, *Fin-de-siècle Vienna*, 72–74.
15   Ibid., 10.
16   Ibid., 11–12, 25–26. Quotes taken from p. 11.
17   Schorske, *Fin-de-siècle Vienna*, 74–83.
18   Sarnitz, *Otto Wagner*, 13.
19   Ibid., 33–34.
20   Ibid., 37.
21   Schorske, *Fin-de-siècle Vienna*, 74–83.
22   Sarnitz, *Otto Wagner*, 47–50.
23   Quoted in Jane Kallir, *Vienna Design and the Wiener Werkstätte* (New York: George Braziller, 1986), 16–17.
24   Ibid., 19.
25   Schorske, *Fin-de-siècle Vienna*, 85. See also G. Fahr-Becker, *L'Art Nouveau* (Königswinter: H. F. Ullmann, 2015), 335–381.
26   Sarnitz, *Otto Wagner*, 15
27   Ibid., 12–13.
28   Ibid., 49.
29   For more images and a detailed description see https://en.wikiarqui tectura.com/building/apartment-building-in-linke-wienzeile-and-koestler gasse-1/.
30   Sarnitz, *Otto Wagner*, 48; Schorske, *Fin-de-siècle Vienna*, 86.
31   Schorske, *Fin-de-siècle Vienna*, 87.
32   Ibid.
33   Ibid., 91.
34   Ibid., 87.
35   Ibid., 87–95.
36   Ibid., 95–101.
37   Sarnitz, *Otto Wagner*, 47–50. In pictures, Baroness Leonie von Puttkamer is seen posing for the camera dressed in the 1920s upper-class bohemian style with furs, and often accompanied by her dog. For context on her outlook, see Thomas Bleitner, *Women of the 1920s: Style, Glamour, and the Avant-Garde* (New York: Abbeville Press, 2019). On the figure of the coquette, prostitution, and the New Woman more broadly, see Jill Suzanne Smith, *Berlin Coquette: Prostitution and the New German Woman, 1890–1933* (Ithaca, NY: Cornell University Press, 2003). See also Gemma Blackshaw, ed., *Facing the Modern: The Portrait in Vienna 1900* (London: National Gallery, 2013).
38   Rieder and Voigt, *The Story of Sidonie C.*, 9–10.
39   This particular station was closed during the First World War and reopened only in 1925 as part of the new Vienna Electric Light Rail and the modernization and electrification of the Stadtbahn. Gretl may well have used the stop until it closed, or she may have misremembered it closing, though her memory of the location was correct.
40   https://commons.wikimedia.org/wiki/File:Wien_-_Majolika-Haus.JPG. This file is licensed under the Creative Commons Attribution-Share Alike 4.0 International license and the author is Greymouser.
41   https://commons.wikimedia.org/wiki/File:194L09160590_Stadt,_Linke_ Wienzeile,_Otto_Wagner,_Haus.jpg. According to the link, "The

copyright holder of this file, TARS631, allows anyone to use it for any purpose, provided that the copyright holder is properly attributed. Redistribution, derivative work, commercial use, and all other use is permitted. Attribution: TARS631."

42 Cf. Judith R. Walkowitz, "Going Public: Shopping, Street Harassment, and Streetwalking in Late Victorian London," *Representations* no. 62 (1998): 1–30.

43 Rieder and Voigt, *The Story of Sidonie C.*, 10.

44 https://sammlung.wienmuseum.at/objekt/135150-innenansicht-des-alten-cafe -dobner-6-linke-wienzeile-2getreidemarkt-1-kaffeehausgaeste-zeitungsleser- ober-kellner/.

45 Schorske, *Fin-de-siècle Vienna*, 82–85.

46 Rieder and Voigt, *The Story of Sidonie C.*, 12. Cf. Deborah Cohen, *The War Come Home: Disabled Veterans in Britain and Germany, 1914–1939* (Berkeley: University of California Press, 2001).

47 For details of the Café Dobner, see https://www.geschichtewiki.wien.gv. at/Café_Dobner.

48 Alexander von Vegesack, *Thonet: Classic Furniture in Bent Wood and Tubular Steel* (New York: Rizzoli, 1997).

49 Rieder and Voigt, *The Story of Sidonie C.*, 12.

50 Ibid., 14.

51 Sigmund Freud, "The Psychogenesis of a Case of Homosexuality in a Woman," *The Standard Edition of the Complete Psychological Works of Sigmund Freud*, ed. J. Strachey (London: Hogarth Press, 1920), vol. 18, 162. From here on, in this section too, *The Standard Edition* is referred to as *SE* with the volume number, date and page number(s) only.

52 Ibid., 154. Freud added, "in her behaviour to her adored lady the girl had adopted the characteristic masculine type of love. Her humility and her tender lack of pretensions, 'che poco spera e nulla chiede' ['Hoping little and asking for nothing'], her bliss when she was allowed to accompany the lady a little way and to kiss her hand on parting, her joy when she heard her praised as beautiful (while any recognition of her own beauty by another person meant nothing at all to her), her pilgrimages to places once visited by the loved one, the silence of all more sensual wishes—all these little traits in her resembled the first passionate adoration of a youth for a celebrated actress whom he regards as far above him, to whom he scarcely dares lift his bashful eyes." Ibid., 160.

53 Ibid., 162.

54 A footnote added here to the text is helpful: "[In the text there is a play on the word niederkommen, which means both 'to fall' and 'to be delivered of a child'. There is in English, too, a colloquial use of the verb 'to fall', meaning pregnancy or childbirth.]—That the various methods of suicide can represent sexual wish-fulfilments has long been known to all analysts. (To poison oneself = to become pregnant; to drown = to bear a child; to throw oneself from a height = to be delivered of a child.)" Ibid., 162, n. 1.

55 Ibid., 162.

56 Ibid., 164.

57 Ibid.

58   Lang and Sutton do mention that the bond between analyst and patient is crucial to the success of the analysis. Yet in discussing Dora's case as an example, they over-stress the idea that the analyst's voice becomes dominant in contrast with the confessional nature of the analytic sessions. To the authors, this occurred in ways that underlined the analyst's close knowledge of his patient and the fact that he even valued her contribution. Birgit Lang and Katie Sutton, "The Queer Cases of Psychoanalysis: Rethinking the Scientific Study of Homosexuality, 1890s–1920s," *German History* 34, no. 3 (September 2016): 420, 425.

59   Rieder and Voigt, *The Story of Sidonie C.*, 14. All quotes recorded by her biographers were taken in retrospective many years after the fact, but alas this is what we have as a testimony to the events.

60   Ibid.

61   See Martha Vicinus, *Intimate Friends: Women Who Loved Women, 1778–1929* (Chicago: University of Chicago Press, 2004). A different reading emphasizes that the cultural presence of the female invert was marked primarily in terms of gender transgression (such as seen among feminists who turned to "mannish" pursuits like literary endeavors, wearing trousers, or smoking), rather than by assumption about sexual behaviors, see Heike Bauer, *English Literary Sexology: Translations of Inversion, 1860–1930* (New York: Palgrave Macmillan, 2009), 1–20. Indeed, it is interesting that in her performance and dress, or in her later profession, Csonka did not adopt a more masculine attire or occupation.

62   In fact, Ungargasse intersects with Strohgasse and Neulinggasse, where the Csonka family lived in 1910.

63   Paul Reitter, *Bambi's Jewish Roots and Other Essays on German-Jewish Culture* (London: Bloomsbury, 2015).

64   Rieder and Voigt, *The Story of Sidonie C.*, 23. The title in the original German is *Josefine Mutzenbacher oder die Geschichte einer Wienerischen Dirne von ihr selbst erzählt.*

65   Kreis Regenwalde was renamed Ustronie Morskie and today is in Poland. Leonie von Puttkamer's death certificate no. 1579 was issued on May 26, 1953, in Charlottenburg, Berlin. The certificate states that on her death on May 23, 1953, Leonie was a language instructor, residing at Altenburger Allee 19, Charlottenburg. The certificate mentions heart failure and a brain tumor as the causes of death. Landesarchiv Berlin; Personenstandsregister Sterberegister; Laufendenummer, 137, accessed via www.ancestry.com. During the 1930s and 1940s, Leonie lived at the following addresses: 2 Xantener Str., Westenedallee 64, Amtliches Fernsprechbuch für den Bezirk der Reichspostdirektion Berlin for the years 1937/8/9/, Berlin Central and Regional Library. (See Figure 8).

66   Taufen, Evangelische Kirche, Militärgemeinde Düsseldorf, 1865, entry no. 18 for Anna Louise von Alvensleben, born July 30, 1865; Evangelisches Kirchenbuchamt Hannover; Film Number: 492467, accessed via www.ancestry.com. Anna Louise died on July 19, 1945 in Florence, Italy, see the entry for Anna Louise von Alvensleben von Holnstein at www.findagrave.com.

67   Deaths, 1906–1921, Berlin, Brandenburg Military Records, vol: B515, 147, entry no. 7 for Werner Alvensleben, died February 8, 1912.

68 Death, 1895–1905, Berlin, Brandenburg Military Record, vol: B533, 146, entry no. 6 for Hermine Freiin von Alvensleben née von Nagell.

69 See Handbuch des Preussischen Adels (Berlin, 1892), 6, article 4. b. The source provides the entire family lineage of the Alvensleben nobility.

70 Günther Georg Peter von Puttkamer (March 27, 1861, Schlackow, Saleske, Pommern – January 12, 1921, Baden, Baden, Germany) Königlichen Kammerjunker of Schlackow (today Złakowo, Poland) and Lieutenant of the Reserve in the Hussar Regiment no.3 of the Prussian Army (Husaren-Regiment von Zieten, Brandenburg). See *Johanniter-Ordensblatt: Amtliche Monatschrift der Balley Brandenburg,* May 10, 1893, 109 (Berlin: Karl Lehmans Verlag, 1893), and n. 279 (reference containing his exact birthdate), and www.ancestry.com, Baden and Hesse Germany, Lutheran Baptisms, Marriages, and Burials, 1502–1985.

71 Heiratsregister; Personenstandsregister, Laufendenummer: 200, Landesarchiv Berlin, marriage certificate no. 746 on the marriage of Juliana Anna Erike von Puttkamer and Alfred Eduard Joseph Dyckhoff.

72 As no record confirming Agathon's birthdate was located, the date is based on the family tree at www.ancestry.com. The fact that Leonie had a brother of that name is confirmed by later findings (see note 76), and is also mentioned in Rieder and Voigt, *The Story of Sidonie C.,* 64.

73 The Berlin court accepted Günther's accusation of adultery on the part of Anna Louise, depriving her of the right to her children and limiting her visits to them to only once a year. See "Feindliche Aristokraten," *Neues Wiener Journal,* April 25, 1913, 11.

74 *Genealogisches Taschenbuch der Adeligen Häuser Österreichs* (Vienna: Otto Maaß' Söhne Verlag, 1905), 496. The marriage was also announced in the Vienna weekly *Sport und Salon,* October 10, 1904, 7.

75 Rieder and Voigt, *The Story of Sidonie C.,* 66.

76 Marquis of Ruvginy, *The Titled Nobility of Europe: An International Peerage,* entry for Holnstein aus Bayren (London, 1914), 793; and *Gothaisches genealogisches Taschenbuch der gräflichen Häuser,* Teil B, v.112, (Justues Perthes, 1939), 221. On October 8, 1912, Anna Louise's second husband, Count Ludwig Karl von Holnstein, physically assaulted her first husband, Count Puttkamer, in the Marne spa resort, where Puttkamer and his second wife stayed. Shortly afterwards, Holnstein made his version of the event public through the Berlin and Munich press (see, for instance, *Neues Wiener Journal,* October 11, 1912, 8, and the *Salzburger Chronik,* October 11, 1912, 5). He accused Puttkamer of having insulted his wife, and portrayed his assault as the result of the injustice he had suffered by the military court (Miltärische Ehrenrat) and other legal tribunals, which had ruled for the peaceful settlement of the conflict (that is, against a duel), much to his dismay. The incident and the public accusations ultimately led Puttkamer to file a lawsuit, and to a highly publicized trial ("Eine Skandalaffäre aus der deutschen Aristokratie," so ran the title in the *Salzburger Volksblatt,* April 25, 1913, 11). Leonie herself was brought as a witness, where she confirmed that her brother, Agathon, had sent her a letter with defamatory messages concerning her mother and Count Holnstein. The press coverage also mentions that when Leonie came of age, she met her mother in London, without her father's knowledge (*Die Zeit,* April 24, 1913, 3).

possibly marking her separation from him in favor of her mother. (In this regard, see also Rieder and Voigt, *The Story of Sidonie C.*, 66.) For concluding coverage of the affair, see "Feindliche Aristokraten," *Neues Wiener Journal*, April 25, 1913, 11.

77   Gretl's biographers mention a conversation in which Leonie told Gretl about her childhood in the castle. See Rieder and Voigt, *The Story of Sidonie C.*, 22.

78   Ibid., 62–66.

79   Ibid., 24.

80   Ibid., 25.

81   In ways that put a more positive spin on Georg Simmel's attempts to articulate the inner meaning of modern aspects of contemporary urban life in his classic, "The Metropolis and Mental Life," in *The Blackwell City Reader*, ed. Gary Bridge and Sophie Watson (Oxford: Wiley-Blackwell, 2010), 103–110.

82   Rieder and Voigt, *The Story of Sidonie C.*, 26. Indeed, as the war ended and inflation raged, Freud welcomed patients who, like Gretl's father, could pay in foreign currency.

83   Ibid., 26.

84   Ibid., 27. These are paraphrases documented by her biographers.

85   Ibid., 27, paraphrased.

86   Ibid., 29, paraphrased.

87   Ibid., 29.

88   Ibid., 29.

89   Ibid., 32.

90   Lacking any birth records, the exact birthdate was calculated on the basis of Csonka's profile on the official Vienna cemeteries website.

91   Geburtsbuch der Israelitischen Kultusgemeinde Wien (IKG), F. 1874–1877, entry N.3000 for Irma Kern, born February 19, 1876. Archival signature: A/VIE/IKG/I/BUCH/MA/GEBURTSBCUH/33, accessed via www.familysearch.org.

92   The names Rika and Rebeka are used alternately in official registrations, as is apparent from additional records listed below.

93   Vienna Deaths Vol. D, N. 26, www.jewishgen.org, entry for Kern - Berger Rika, January 8, 1887. The record states that she was originally from Szegedin (the German name for the Hungarian city Szeged), where the Jewish population in 1880 totalled 3,618. (Data taken from the Communities Database at www.jewishgen.org). Thus, like her husband, Irma was of Jewish-Hungarian extraction, as confirmed by additional registrations and records listed in the footnotes below.

94   Her father's profession is mentioned in Irma's birth record (see note 91) and in the burial registry entry on www.jewishgen.org for Emanuel Kern, buried October 10, 1891. NB: there is a mistake in the transcribed death age, as he died at the age of 56–58, not 33. This is also mentioned in his entry in the Vienna Death, V. F., N. 480, www.jewishgen.org, and is supported by the information in his marriage registration (see note 95). The death record further states that he was originally from Nebowid (present-day Nebovidy, Czech Republic).

95   Hungarian Marriage, LDS 642786, Vol. 3, 50–08, www.jewishgen.org, entry for Rebeka Berger and Mano Kern, January 13, 1869.

96 Hungarian Births, LDS 642785, Vol. 2, www.jewishgen.org, entry for Hugo Kern, May 1, 1870.

97 Vienna Births, E1 1870–72, Vol. E, Nu. 3935, www.jewishgen.org, entry for Viktor Kern, September 9, 1872. According to Gretl's biographers, Viktor was killed in the First World War.

98 Vienna Births, E2 1872–74, Vol. E, Nu. 6118, Vienna IKG, www.jewish gen.org, entry for Josephine Kern, October 8, 1873. From these birth registrations, one learns that the Kerns moved to Vienna after their first child and before their second was born, c.1871.

99 Possibly Jozef Bergi, Irma's witness at her wedding according to their marriage registration (see note 108), who, like Irma's mother, was from Szeged (Kiskundorozsma village).

100 Israelitische Kirche Geburtsregister, 1820–1877, Buda-Neolog, Vol. 1., 1869, 209, entry no. 90 for Moricz Abroham Arpad / Moshe Avraham Csonka, October 2, 1896, FHL microfilm 642,991. According to Arpad's birth record, the name Arpad was added in 1888. See original record at www.familysearch.org.

101 Archiv der Stadt Budapest, Hungary, Deaths registrations, entry no.1858/I, 316, for Csonka Ignác, July 13, 1899, accessed via www.fam ilysearch.org.

102 Budapest Civil and Housing Register for 1894 (8th year) part 6, 496, entry for "Csonka Ign," accessed via www.Genealogyindexer.org The document also contains entries for Arpad and his elder brother Sandor. All three were residing at the same address, Lanczhid u-6, which is also mentioned as Arpad's address on his marriage certificate (see note 108).

103 Israelitische Kirche Geburtsregister, 1820–1877, Buda-Neolog, Vol. 1, 179, entry no. 80 for Sandor Csonka, 1867, Magyar Orszagos Leveltar (Hungarian National Archives), FHL microfilm 642, 991. Via www.fam ilysearch.org. Sandor was a tailor (see reference in note 102). On September 4, 1898, he married Malvine Müller (1878) from Bonyhád (Hungarian Marriages, www.jewishgen.org, September 4, 1898).

104 Deaths, Budapest, Archiv der Stadt Budapest, entry no. 428, 86, Aranka Elbert née Csonka, March 21, 1953. Accessed via www.familysearch.org "Hungary Civil Registration, 1895–1980." She married Mano Elbert in 1895 (see Marriages, entry no. 49, 17), and had at least one child, Ladislaus Elbert. During the Holocaust, Ladislaus managed to gain a "Wallenberg passport" (no. 8311, case 4059). See the Wallenberg List database at www.jewishgen.org.

105 Israelitische Kirche Geburtsregister, 1820–1877, Buda-Neolog, Vol. 1., 1871, entry no. 96, 229, for Malvine/Matel, Magyar Orszagos Leveltar (Hungarian National Archives), Hungary; FHL microfilm 642, 991.

106 Roman Sandgruber, *Traumzeit für Millionäre: Die 929 reichsten Wienerinnen und Wiener im Jahr 1910* (Vienna: Styria, 2013), 325.

107 See Alison Fleig Frank, *Oil Empire: Visions of Prosperity in Austrian Galicia* (Cambridge, MA: Harvard University Press, 2007).

108 Marriages, 1897, 229, entry no. 740 for Arpad Csonka and Irma Kern, married October 31, 1897, Archiv der Stadt Budapest (Archive of the City), Hungary, www.familysearch.org.

109 During the Second World War, two ghettos were formed in Boryslav, one of which was for workers in the oil industry. The Germans and local

Ukrainians murdered Jews en masse in Boryslav and the surrounding area. See Geoffrey P. Megargee and Martin Dean, eds., *Encyclopedia of Camps and Ghettos*, vol. 2 (Bloomington: University of Indiana Press, 2012), 755–757. Hans/Johannes Csonka (born May 21, 1899, died June 15, 1977), son of Arpad Csonka, became an engineer. Following Arpad's death in 1934, he took control of his father's companies. During the Second World War, he lived in Paris where, following the Nazi occupation, he hid with a French family friend for more than three years. After the war, Hans (also known in Paris as Jean) remained in Paris, residing at 46 Rue Raymond Poincaré, 16e. In 1956, with the support of the Austrian embassy, Hans founded and presided over the Austrian Association in Paris (Österreichische Vereinigung in Paris)—the Paris branch of the Auslandösterreichischer Weltbund (AÖWB—Association of Austrians Abroad). Hans died at the age of 78 in Spain. For further information, see Wolfgang Schallenberg, "Erinnerungen an die Gründung," published in a brochure marking 60 years of the founding of the Austrian Association in Paris, 18–19; file FLD 6.247, Ing. Hans Csonka, Austrian State Archives, "France, Indice de décès de la sécurité sociale de l'Insee, 1970–2019," www.familysearch.org Johannes Csonka, 1977.

110   Deaths, Archiv der Stadt Budapest, Hungary, entry no. 119 for Schulhof Berta, March 19, 1923, accessed via www.familysearch.org.

111   William O. McCagg, *A History of Habsburg Jews, 1670–1918* (Bloomington: Indiana University Press, 1989).

112   Archiv der Erzdiözese Wien; Wien, Österreich; Katholische Kirchenbücher; Pfarre: St Karl Borromaeus; Signatur: 9037; Laufendenummer: 01–28, entry for Paul August Csonka born October 24, 1905, via www.ancestry.com. NB: There is a mistake in the transcription of the birth year (it was not 1903). Paul died on November 24, 1995, in Palm Beach, Florida. There, in 1962, he had been appointed creative director of the Civic Opera of the Palm Beaches, which ultimately became the Palm Beach Opera, which he led for over two decades (based partially on his obituary, "Paul Csonka, Community Opera Leader," *South Florida Sun Sentinel*, November 26, 1995).

113   Archiv der Erzdiözese Wien; Wien, Österreich; Katholische Kirchenbücher; Pfarre: Landstrasse-St Rochus; Signatur: 9025; Laufendenummer: 01–87; entry for Alexander Walter Csonka, born June 7, 1917, via www.ancestry.com. On September 19, 1938, Alexander left Vienna and fled from the Nazis to Cuba three days later, settling in Havana at Calle 13 Entre Avenida, 1a. y. 2a. Ampliacion De Almendares, Marianao (file VA.7.859, Austrian State Archives). There he married Marta Hoyos in 1955; they divorced on April 30, 1999. In 1956, he arrived in the USA, settling in Miami, Florida, where he was ultimately naturalized in 1961. He died in Miami on June 11, 2009 at the age of 92.

114   Rieder and Voigt, *The Story of Sidonie C.*, 33, paraphrased.

115   See Steven Frosh, *Hate and the "Jewish Science": Anti-Semitism, Nazism and Psychoanalysis* (New York: Palgrave Macmillan, 2005), 9–32.

116   Rieder and Voigt, *The Story of Sidonie C.*, 33–34.

117   See, for example, ibid., 254, 269, 345, 256. Without essentializing the fact that Gretl was born Jewish, I discuss her life beyond her personal fraught relationship with her background and the fact that she was

baptized (to flee from antisemitism), in the context of the conditions of assimilated or acculturated Jewish life between equality and racism, her family's background, and her fate throughout the twentieth century that was typical of many Central European Jewish women. She had a conflicted Jewish identification (which was characteristic of many Jews at the time when they were seen as outsiders in Vienna). But the fact that she was of Jewish descent meant that she had to negotiate the cultural and social meanings of her "Jewishness," or how it was viewed from the outside by gentiles. She began looking at it "from the inside" and engaging with her family history thanks to Freud. In short, I discuss her beyond her personal, shifting identifications as socially and culturally we can view her in part as a second-generation assimilated Jew.

118 Rieder and Voigt, *The Story of Sidonie C.*, 38.
119 Ibid., 42.
120 Ibid.
121 The owner, Béla Waldmann, was Jewish and the café was confiscated and then fell into decline when the Nazis took over in 1938. Waldmann, however, survived the war. Birgit Schwaner, *The Viennese Coffee House: Legend, Culture, Atmosphere* (Vienna: Pichler Verlag, 2007), 165–181. In 1938, Fayans was banned from practicing his profession and he was eventually murdered by Germans in 1942. See Ursula Prokop, *Zum jüdischen Erbe in der Wiener Architektur. Der Beitrag jüdischer ArchitektInnen am Wiener Baugeschehen 1868–1938* (Vienna: Böhlau, 2016), 218–219.
122 See Smith, *Berlin Coquette*.
123 For the interior of the café see https://www.geschichtewiki.wien.gv.at/Caf%C3%A9_Herrenhof.
124 Or at least this is how she remembered it when she recited these words and recalled the incident years later to her biographers (see note 3). See Rieder and Voigt, *The Story of Sidonie C.*, 45; emphasis in the original.
125 Ibid., 45.
126 Ibid., 46–49.
127 Known then for its "First Class Lady's Hairdressing and Manicure," Salon Geppert was located at 4 Kruger Straße.
128 Rieder and Voigt, *The Story of Sidonie C.*, 49
129 Ibid., 55.
130 Ibid., xi.
131 In a manner that both parallels and contradicts her father's broken promise to his mother regarding the preservation of Judaism in the family, Gretl broke her promise to her father that she would become heterosexual. Gretl also deliberately chose as her beloved a liminal figure in terms of class, and a non-Jewish, older woman who increased her chances of being ostracized and shunned by society, and further damage the family's name.

Conclusion

The relatively neglected 1920 case of female homosexuality was often seen as revealing a conventional, phallocentric Freud who could not think of desire in non-masculine terms. He equated worldly behavior and sexual activity with masculinity, and passivity with femininity, and saw activity in women as a masculine complex; he viewed hetero-sexuality as the end goal of sexual development, and abruptly had to terminate the analysis of this young female homosexual sent to him by her parents. Indeed, this was not his first, but his second failed case of a young woman homosexual in love. In the earlier case of Dora, it was she who left the analysis, whereas the 1920 case was terminated by Freud. Nonetheless, there is an unresolved tension in Freud's own life and in his writings on femininity, for he was both patronizing and a traditional Victorian conservative in his convictions and prejudices about women, yet he was also a man who welcomed women to the profession of psychoanalysis, and he was willing to question and fundamentally challenge the sexual mores of the time.[1]

Thus, in the first part of this book I revealed and emphasized the radical edge of the 1920 paper on female homosexuality by offering a historical reading of the text in context, and stressing the more radical elements of his work—better known perhaps for his views on male homosexuality—in comparison with other medical men, and in the context of his developing views on homosexuality. I showed that Freud did not see the young woman's homosexuality as a problem per se; he did not treat homosexuality in a derogatory manner, nor did he try to cure her of it. He did not see her as ill, neurotic, or degenerate. He also wanted to redirect the question of nature versus nurture and argued that, more than anything, homosexuality was a choice made as part of psychosexual development in ways not dissimilar to hetero-sexuality. When discussing her inversion, he did not suggest a third sex/physical condition theory (like some other sexologists of the

DOI: 10.4324/9781003352662-4

period); rather, he contended that she had mentally adopted a specific gendered norm or "a psychological attitude." This in itself should change our perception of the text as being more open-ended than some have perceived. In this Freud moved the discussion to the field of "psychological inversion" rather than keeping it as "bodily inversion."[2] As a Jewish man, his ideas about homophobia and homosexuality were influenced by antisemitism. In all this, he was radical for his time, and he also advanced ideas already put forward by some of his contemporaries. He was offering a broader theory of sexuality than the sexologists, emphasizing internal family relationships.

Revisionist scholarship on the sexologists' attitudes to homosexuality demonstrated that their ideas shifted and changed over time, and presented both contradiction and complexity. Yet, at the same time, this scholarship seems to tone down Freud's innovation and overstress how those who preceded him foreshadowed many of his ideas. I suggested that we take a more balanced view as we integrate the important revisionist findings about the sexologists without disregarding Freud's distinct contribution to the debate on homosexuality. Thus, despite the fact that Freud was not as revolutionary as he himself argued, placing his ideas and analyzing and scrutinizing them closely in the context of the medical discourse of the time, and of the prevailing antisemitism, still shows the uniqueness of his voice and how he was more radical for his time than later feminists remembered him.

The second part of the book deals with the analytic treatment as seen through the eyes of the young woman patient we now know as Margarethe (Gretl) Csonka. It places her in the wide context of changes in the fields of urban development, cultural languages of love, and ethnic relations in Vienna, and juxtaposes her narrative with that of Freud. It situates the love affair within the context of the modern culture of Vienna beyond the medical world and its discourse. The city, its architecture, and its institutions allowed Gretl and Baroness Leonie von Puttkamer the freedom to meet and visit the new sites as two modern New Women. The city streets, buildings, cafés, interior design, phone booths, and public transportation served as a backdrop to, and facilitator of, their relationship. So did the romantic codes of conduct (usually available to heterosexual men) for actively courting a lover that Csonka reworked to express her same-sex desire. This part of the book also stresses that not only was Freud Jewish, so was his patient in terms of her background. I anchored them as assimilated Jews and situated their relationship further in the context of modern Jewish life in a society and culture vacillating between emancipatory rights and antisemitic racism.

The book points to moments of dialogue and resistance between Freud and Csonka, for instance regarding Csonka's reworking of heterosexual models of romance and chivalry, or her and Freud's navigation of Jewish identity, assimilation, and antisemitic prejudice. Freud invited Gretl to rewrite her state of being, her thoughts, and inner feelings, to look back at her history as he provided a modern framework for introspection, self-contemplation, and self-narration of her personal, ethnic, and family autobiography together with him (more than the sexologists would have done). Her sexuality was privileged as the seat of her individuality vis-à-vis her family and social mores. But Csonka rejected much of the specific path offered by Freud, as well as the inner logic of his explanation for her self-awareness and self-expression of her love for women. Unlike other sexologists' patients, correspondents, and informants, who tried to appropriate sexological logic for their own purposes, or to persuade professional psychiatrists that they were healthy, Csonka withdrew from treatment with Freud and did not try to argue with him or persuade him. Yet it cannot be said that their meetings were entirely fruitless because she gained the insight and technique that linked her individual introspection with sexual and ethnic identity; thus, perhaps she was better able to narrate her life in a continuous process of self-discovery that may have given her the courage to pursue same-sex love. Furthermore, both Freud and Csonka as a young woman rejected traditional patterns of sexuality, but in different ways. Rather than adopting a traditional view of sexuality—as primarily embedded in a fixed, natural, moral, and familiar order, or as marriage, reproduction, stable gender roles and social, economic, and ethnic concerns—they both paid more attention to a modern, individual preoccupation with personal desires, life stories, and attraction. Both downplayed moral and economic concerns. For both, personal desire was at the center and sexuality became a key sphere of human life, personal fulfilment, and the expression of authenticity in contrast to social mores. Through their meeting of minds, sexual variation became more closely tied to personal identity as an important characteristic of sexual modernity.[3] Their encounter against the backdrop of the fluctuating racist and homophobic conditions prevailing in Vienna at the time, and in the context of other medical and changing urban, social, and ethnic-religious realities of the interwar period, help us to better understand homosexual female desire through the lens of both medical and non-medical ideas. This also enables a better understanding of the history of female sexuality which nonetheless still remained understudied.

Though Csonka struggled with her sexuality throughout her life and had to marry and ultimately divorce a man she disliked, she continued to have women lovers and loved (or just fantasized about) them passionately. She found it hard to sustain intimacy, but never wanted anything but homosexual love. Her Jewishness, however, remained more conflicted for her. Unfortunately, her story mirrored that of other Jews in Europe in the mid-twentieth century, though she was one of the very few—several thousand out of a Jewish population of close to 180,000 in Vienna in 1938—who survived the war. Following Nazi Germany's invasion of Austria, she became a refugee. She was forced to flee from Vienna to Moscow, Russia, and took the Trans-Siberian railroad to Japan, crossing the ocean to North America, and eventually spending the war in Havana, Cuba.

Die verhaftete Frau Geßmann-Puttkammer.

Figure 17 A drawing of Leonie von Puttkamer dressed in prison uniform
Source: *Montag mit dem Sport-Montag*, March 31, 1924, 2.

Csonka's relationship with Leonie von Puttkamer continued in the 1920s as a close friendship. In 1924, the baroness found herself embroiled in a legal and medical scandal, and in a fight against her husband, Albert Gessman Jr., whose doctor had filed a complaint with the police claiming that he had found traces of arsenic in Albert's coffee, after Albert had told him he was feeling unwell. On March 28, 1924, Leonie arrived for questioning by the police and was subsequently arrested at the Regional Courthouse (Landesgericht) on suspicion of attempted murder by spiking Gessman's coffee with arsenic on the night of March 19–20. On the following day, after Gessman and Gretl (identifying herself as Leonie's closest friend) were questioned, the public prosecutor's office (Staatsanwaltschaft) charged

Figure 18 Photograph of Paul, Margarethe and Hans Csonka, with their mother Irma after the war, in Algeciras, Spain, 1966
Source: Freud Museum archive, Vienna, Sigmund-Freud-Privatstiftung.

Leonie with attempted murder. The prosecutor also ordered a court interrogation into "when and where she had sexual intercourse with Anita Berber, Carola Horn [and] Bebbi Becker," among other women, under paragraph 129 of the Austrian criminal code, and decreed that Leonie should undergo psychiatric examination.[4] By early April, Leonie was cleared of the attempted murder charge, and the court moved to focus mainly on her lesbian relationships. As part of these proceedings, Leonie and Albert filed petitions against each other, each claiming that the other was sexually "perverted" and mentally ill.

The affair drew enormous press attention, which extended to Germany.[5] Between March 30–31, reports of the affair caught the

Figure 19 Photograph of Margarethe Csonka after the war, in 1955 together with her beloved dog Petzi in Central Park, New York
Source: Freud Museum archive, Vienna, Sigmund-Freud-Privatstiftung.

headlines of almost all the newspapers in Austria, some devoting their entire front pages to the case which, as *Die Neue Zeitung* stated, "grew into a social scandal, the likes of which Vienna had not seen for a long time."[6] The weekly *Montag mit dem Sport-Montag* went so far as to post an illustration of Leonie dressed in prison uniform (Figure 17).[7]

On October 7, 1924, all charges against Leonie were dropped due to lack of evidence and the fact that most of the illegal acts attributed to her had occurred in Germany, where female homosexuality was not a criminal offense. Leonie left Vienna immediately for Berlin, although the Vienna courts continued to discuss the civil lawsuits the couple had filed well into 1925.[8]

When Gretl was fleeing Nazi-occupied Europe, she managed to stop in Berlin, was reunited after sixteen years with Leonie at no. 2 Xantener Straße,[9] and the two women finally made love.[10] Nine years after the war, Gretl returned to Vienna. She struggled to find work and moved between various rented rooms. She found it hard to adjust to postwar Austrian society since she and her family there had become poor and déclassé (Figures 18 and 19). With help from friends, out of adventure and necessity, she travelled the world working as a governess and housekeeper in Thailand, Brazil, Scarsdale, New York State, and Spain;[11] she also became a painter.

Eventually, Gretl returned to Vienna, and again with the help of friends found a residence for the elderly to her liking,[12] and received a small sum from the Austrian government in compensation as a victim of the Holocaust.[13] She enjoyed the city life once again; she even visited a lesbian bar at the age of ninety-six. She still remembered Freud with a mixture of rage and contempt and enjoyed the fact that she had given him a tough time.[14] She lived to the age of ninety-nine.[15]

Notes

1 Peter Gay, *Freud: A Life for Our Time* (New York: Norton, 2006), 501–522; Elizabeth Grosz, *Space, Time and Perversion* (New York: Routledge, 1995), 160.
2 I thank Gil Engelstein for stressing this point.
3 Cf. the phrasing in Harry Oosterhuis, "Sexual Modernity in the Works of Richard von Krafft-Ebing and Albert Moll," *Medical History* 56, no. 2 (April 2012): 152–155.
4 Ines Rieder and Diana Voigt, eds., *The Story of Sidonie C.: Freud's Famous "Case of Female Homosexuality,"* trans. Jill Hannum and Ines Rieder (Budapest: Helena History Press, 2019), 81–82. It was first published in German in 2000.
5 See for example "Wiener Giftmordaffäre," *Berliner Tageblatt*, March 31, 1924, 3; "Versuchter Giftmord," *Deutsche Allgemeine Zeitung*, March 31,

1924, 3; "Ein Giftvermordsuch in der Wiener Gesellschaft," *Leipziger Tageblatt*, April 1, 1924, 5; "Ein ungeklärte Giftmordversuch in Wien," *Dreseden Neuste Nachrichten*, 17.

6 "Die Giftvermorde Gessman," *Die Neue Zeitung*, April 2, 1924. The article states the exact paragraphs of the criminal code that apply to the charges against Leonie, and mentions Leonie's influence on Csonka's suicide attempt, but it avoids revealing her true identity and refers to her as "das Mädchen" (the girl).

7 "Albert Gessman Wieder Enthaftet," *Montag mit dem Sport-Montag*, March 31, 1924, 2. The article devotes the front and second page to the affair, discussing and analyzing it and the personalities involved in a rather scandalous tone.

8 For a fuller and more detailed account of the case, and Gretl's involvement in it, see Rieder and Voigt, *The Story of Sidonie C.*, 56–106.

9 See note 65 in Part II for Leonie's addresses in Berlin before, during, and after the war and Figure 8.

10 Rieder and Voigt, *The Story of Sidonie C.*, 222–227. The biography is extremely useful for further information on her life.

11 Gretl's mother and brother Hans seem to have passed away in Algeciras in Cádiz, Spain. However, no sufficient evidence supporting this has yet been found. For more on her life, see: Trautenegg, Margarethe von, 1900–1999—Correspondence in Kurt R. Eissler Papers, Box 2, Manuscript Division, Library of Congress, Washington, DC, 1969–88.

12 Based on Gretl's compensation claim file (see note 13), in 1979 or 1980 she moved into the Wiener Frauenheim at Frauenheimgasse 2, 1120 Wien, a residential home for the elderly, established in 1881. For further information about the history of this unique institution, see Frauen in Bewegung, https://fraueninbewegung.onb.ac.at/node/774/12:49.

13 In 1978, Gretl filed a compensation claim (NHF.26.772) to the Fonds zur Hilfeleistung an politisch Verfolgte, die ihren Wohnsitz und ständigen Aufenthalt im Ausland haben (Hilffonds), a statutory organization established in Austria in 1956, entrusted with restitution and reparations for Austrian victims of Nazi persecution. Gretl's mother Irma also filed a claim as early as 1956 (No. 09426) from her residence at 46 Avenue Raymond Poincaré, 16e, Paris, where she lived with her elder son. Access to these files was granted by the Austrian State Archives on the basis of entries found on Findbuch for Victims of National Socialism, an online database containing information on Austrian Holocaust victims and survivors from various sources; see www.findbuch.at.

14 Rieder and Voigt, *The Story of Sidonie C.*, 356–357.

15 She died on August 14, 1999.

Bibliography

Alofsin, Anthony. *When Buildings Speak: Architecture as Language in the Habsburg Empire and Its Aftermath, 1867–1933*. Chicago: Chicago University Press, 2006.

Appignanesi, Lisa, and John Forrester. *Freud's Women*. New York: Other Press, 2001.

Bauer, Heike. *English Literary Sexology: Translations of Inversion, 1860–1930*. New York: Palgrave Macmillan, 2009.

Bauer, Heike. "Theorizing Female Inversion: Sexology, Discipline, and Gender at the Fin de Siècle." *Journal of the History of Sexuality* 18, no. 1 (2009): 84–102.

Beachy, Robert. *Gay Berlin: Birthplace of a Modern Identity*. New York: Knopf, 2014.

Beachy, Robert. "The German Invention of Homosexuality." *The Journal of Modern History* 82, no. 4 (2010): 801–838.

Beccalossi, C. *Female Sexual Inversion: Same-Sex Desires in Italian and British Sexology, c. 1870–1920*. New York: Palgrave Macmillan, 2012.

Bedoire, Fredric. *The Jewish Contribution to Modern Architecture, 1830–1930*. Jersey City, NJ: Ktav Publishing House, 2004.

Beller, Steven. "'The Jew Belongs in the Coffeehouse': Jews, Central Europe and Modernity." In *The Viennese Café and Fin-de-Siècle Culture*, edited by Charlotte Ashby, Tag Gronberg, and Simon Shaw-Miller, 48–50. New York: Berghahn, 2013.

Beller, Steven. *Vienna and the Jews, 1867–1938: A Cultural History*. Cambridge: Cambridge University Press, 1989.

Berkenkotter, Carol. *Patient Tales: Case Histories and the Uses of Narrative in Psychiatry*. Columbia: University of South Carolina Press, 2008.

Bernheim, Charles, and Claire Kahane, eds. *In Dora's Case: Freud-Hysteria-Feminism*. New York: Columbia University Press, 1990.

Blackshaw, Gemma, ed. *Facing the Modern: The Portrait in Vienna 1900*. London: National Gallery, 2013.

Bleitner, Thomas. *Women of the 1920s: Style, Glamour, and the Avant-Garde*. New York: Abbeville Press, 2019.

Boyarin, Daniel. "Freud's Baby, Fliess's Maybe: Homophobia, Anti-Semitism, and the Invention of Oedipus." *Gay and Lesbian Quarterly* 1 (April 1995): 115–147.

Boyarin, Daniel. *Unheroic Conduct: The Rise of Heterosexuality and the Invention of the Jewish Man*. Berkeley: University of California Press, 1997.

Breger, Claudia. "Feminine Masculinities: Scientific and Literary Representations of 'Female Inversion' at the Turn of the Twentieth Century." *Journal of the History of Sexuality* 14, nos. 1–2 (2005): 76–106.

Butler, Judith. *Bodies that Matter: On the Discursive Limits of Sex*. New York: Routledge, 1993.

Chauncey, George. "From Sexual Inversion to Homosexuality: Medicine and the Changing Conceptualization of Female Deviance." *Salmagundi* 58/59 (1982): 114–146.

Cohen, Deborah. *The War Come Home: Disabled Veterans in Britain and Germany, 1914–1939*. Berkeley: University of California Press, 2001.

Dalley Crozier, Ivan "Pillow Talk: Credibility, Trust and the Sexological Case History." *History of Science* 46, no. 4 (2008): 375–404.

Dalley Crozier, Ivan "Taking Prisoners: Havelock Ellis, Sigmund Freud, and the Construction of Homosexuality, 1897–1951." *Social History of Medicine* 13, no. 3 (2000): 450–454.

Dalley Crozier, Ivan "The Medical Construction of Homosexuality and its Relation to the Law in Nineteenth-Century England." *Medical History* 45, no. 1 (2001): 61–82.

Davidson, Arnold Ivan "How to Do the History of Psychoanalysis: A Reading of Freud's 'Three Essays on the Theory of Sexuality.'" *Critical Inquiry* 13, no. 2 (1987): 252–277.

Dean, Tim, and Christopher Lane. *Homosexuality and Psychoanalysis*. Chicago: University of Chicago Press, 2001.

Deutsch, Helene. "On Female Homosexuality." *Psychoanalytic Quarterly* 1 (1932): 484–510.

Doan, Laura. *Fashioning Sapphism: The Origins of a Modern Lesbian Culture*. New York: Columbia University Press, 2000.

Ellis, Havelock. "Sexual Inversion in Women." *Alienist and Neurologist* 16 (1895): 141–158.

Faderman, Lillian. *Surpassing the Love of Men: Romantic Friendship and Love between Women from the Renaissance to the Present*. London: Junction, 1981.

Flanders, S., F. Ladame, A. Carlsberg, P. Heymanns, D. Naziri, and D. Panitz. "On the Subject of Homosexuality: What Freud Said." *International Journal of Psychoanalysis* 97, no. 3 (2016): 933–950.

Fleig Frank, Alison. *Oil Empire: Visions of Prosperity in Austrian Galicia*. Cambridge, MA: Harvard University Press, 2007.

Forrester, John. "If p, Then What? Thinking in Cases." *History of the Human Sciences* 9, no. 1 (1996): 1–25.

Freud, Sigmund. "Analysis of a Phobia in a Five-Year-Old Boy." *The Standard Edition of the Complete Psychological Works of Sigmund Freud*, vol. 10, 1–150, edited by J. Strachey. London: Hogarth Press, 1909.

Freud, Sigmund. "Fragment of an Analysis of a Case of Hysteria." *The Standard Edition of the Complete Psychological Works of Sigmund Freud*, vol. 7, 1–122, edited by J. Strachey. London: Hogarth Press, 1905.

Freud, Sigmund. "From the History of an Infantile Neurosis." *The Standard Edition of the Complete Psychological Works of Sigmund Freud*, vol. 17, 1–124, edited by J. Strachey. London: Hogarth Press, 1911.

Freud, Sigmund. "Leonardo da Vinci and a Memory of his Childhood." *The Standard Edition of the Complete Psychological Works of Sigmund Freud*, vol. 11, 57–138, edited by J. Strachey. London: Hogarth Press, 1910.

Freud, Sigmund. "Letter to an American Mother." *American Journal of Psychiatry* 107 (1951).

Freud, Sigmund. "Notes upon a Case of Obsessional Neurosis." *The Standard Edition of the Complete Psychological Works of Sigmund Freud*, vol. 10, 151–318, edited by J. Strachey. London: Hogarth Press, 1909.

Freud, Sigmund. "On Narcissism: An Introduction." *The Standard Edition of the Complete Psychological Works of Sigmund Freud*, vol. 14, 67–102, edited by J. Strachey. London: Hogarth Press, 1914.

Freud, Sigmund. "Psycho-Analytic Notes on an Autobiographical Account of a Case of Paranoia (Dementia Paranoides)." *The Standard Edition of the Complete Psychological Works of Sigmund Freud*, vol. 12, 1–82, edited by J. Strachey. London: Hogarth Press, 1911.

Freud, Sigmund. "Some Neurotic Mechanisms in Jealousy, Paranoia and Homosexuality." *The Standard Edition of the Complete Psychological Works of Sigmund Freud*, vol. 18, 221–232, edited by J. Strachey. London: Hogarth Press, 1922.

Freud, Sigmund. "Some Psychical Consequences of the Anatomical Distinction between the Sexes." *The Standard Edition of the Complete Psychological Works of Sigmund Freud*, vol. 19, 241–258, edited by J. Strachey. London: Hogarth Press, 1925.

Freud, Sigmund. "The Psychogenesis of a Case of Female Homosexuality." *International Journal of Psychoanalysis* 1, no. 2 (1920).

Freud, Sigmund. "The Psychogenesis of a Case of Homosexuality in a Woman." *The Standard Edition of the Complete Psychological Works of Sigmund Freud*, vol. 18, 145–172, edited by J. Strachey. London: Hogarth Press, 1920.

Freud, Sigmund. "Three Essays on the Theory of Sexuality." *The Standard Edition of the Complete Psychological Works of Sigmund Freud*, vol. 7, 123–246, edited by J. Strachey. London: Hogarth Press, 1905.

Frosh, Steven. *Hate and the 'Jewish Science': Anti-Semitism, Nazism and Psychoanalysis*. New York: Palgrave Macmillan, 2005.

Fuss, Diana. "Fallen Woman: The Psychogenesis of a Case of Homosexuality in a Woman." In *That Obscure Subject of Desire: Freud's Female Homosexual Revisited*, edited by Ronnie C. Lesser and Erica Schoenberg. New York: Routledge, 1999.

Fuss, Diana, ed. "Pink Freud." Special Issue of *GLQ: A Journal of Lesbian and Gay Studies* 2 (1995).

Gay, Peter. *Freud: A Life for Our Time.* New York: Norton, 2006.

Genealogisches Taschenbuch der Adeligen Häuser Österreichs. Vienna: Otto Maaß' Söhne Verlag, 1905.

Gilman, Sander L. *Freud, Race, and Gender.* Princeton, NJ: Princeton University Press, 1993.

Gilman, Sander L. *The Case of Sigmund Freud: Medicine and Identity at the Fin de Siècle.* Princeton, NJ: Princeton University Press, 1993.

Gilman, Sander L. *The Jew's Body.* New York: Routledge, 1991.

Goldstein, Jan. *Hysteria Complicated by Ecstasy: The Case of Nanette Leroux.* Princeton, NJ and Oxford: Princeton University Press, 2011.

Gothaisches genealogisches Taschenbuch der gräflichen Häuser, Part B, vol. 112. Gotha: Justus Perthes, 1939.

Graf, Max. *Composer and Critic: Two Hundred Years of Musical Criticism.* New York: Norton & Company, 1946.

Grigg, Russell. *Female Sexuality: The Early Psychoanalytic Controversies,* edited by Dominique Hecq and Craig Edward Smith. New York: Other Press, 1999.

Gronberg, Tag. *Vienna: City of Modernity, 1890–1914.* Oxford: Peter Lang, 2007.

Grosskurth, Phyllis. *Havelock Ellis: A Biography.* Toronto, ON: McClelland and Stewart, 1980.

Grosz, Elizabeth. *Space, Time and Perversion.* New York: Routledge, 1995.

Hamer, Diane. "Significant Others: Lesbians and Psychoanalytic Theory." *Feminist Review* 34 (Spring 1990): 134–151.

Herzog, Dagmar. *Cold War Freud: Psychoanalysis in an Age of Catastrophes.* Cambridge, MA: Cambridge University Press, 2016.

Irigaray, Luce. "Commodities Among Themselves." In *This Sex Which Is Not One,* translated by Catherine Porter. Ithaca, NY: Cornell University Press, 1985.

Jacobus, Mary. "Russian Tactics: Freud's 'Case of Homosexuality in a Woman.'" In *First Things: Reading the Maternal Imaginary.* New York: Routledge, 1995.

Jennings, Rebecca. *A Lesbian History of Britain: Love and Sex Between Women Since 1500.* Santa Barbara, CA: Greenwood World, 2007.

Jones, Ernest. *Sigmund Freud: Life and Work,* vol. 3: *The Last Phase 1919–1939.* London: Hogarth Press, 1957.

Jones, Ernest. "The Early Development of Female Sexuality." *International Journal of Psycho-Analysis* 8 (1927): 459–472.

Kahan, Benjamin. *The Book of Minor Perverts: Sexology, Etiology, and the Emergence of Sexuality.* Chicago: University of Chicago Press, 2019.

Kallir, Jane. *Vienna Design and the Wiener Werkstätte.* New York: George Braziller, 1986.

Krafft-Ebing, Richard von. *Psychopathia Sexualis: Eine klinisch-forensische Studie,* 1st edn. Stuttgart: Enke, 1886.

Kurimay, Anita. *Queer Budapest, 1873–1961.* Chicago: University of Chicago Press, 2020.

Lang, Birgit. "Normal Enough? Krafft-Ebing, Freud, and Homosexuality." *History of the Human Sciences* 34, no. 2 (2021): 93.

Lang, B., J. Damousi, and A. Lewis. *A History of the Case Study: Sexology, Psychoanalysis, Literature*. Manchester: Manchester University Press, 2017.

Lang, Birgit, and Katie Sutton. "The Queer Cases of Psychoanalysis: Rethinking the Scientific Study of Homosexuality, 1890s–1920s." *German History* 34, no. 3 (September 2016): 419–444.

Lauretis, Teresa de. "Letter to an Unknown Woman." In *That Obscure Subject of Desire*, edited by Ronnie C. Lesser and Erica Schoenberg. New York: Routledge, 1999.

Lauretis, Teresa de. *The Practice of Love: Lesbian Sexuality and Perverse Desire*. Bloomington: Indiana University Press, 1994.

Lesser, Ronnie C. "Introduction." In *That Obscure Subject of Desire*, edited by Ronnie C. Lesser and Erica Schoenberg. New York: Routledge, 1999.

Lybeck, M. M. *Desiring Emancipation: New Women and Homosexuality in Germany, 1890–1933*. New York: State University of New York Press, 2014.

Makari, G. *Revolution in Mind: The Creation of Psychoanalysis*. New York: HarperCollins, 2008.

Marcus, Sharon. *Between Women: Friendship, Desire, and Marriage in Victorian England*. Princeton, NJ and Oxford: Princeton University Press, 2007.

Marquis of Ruvginy, the, ed. "Holnstein aus Bayren." In *The Titled Nobility of Europe: An International Peerage, or "Who's Who," of the Sovereigns, Princes, and Nobles of Europe*. London: Harrison & Sons, 1914.

McCagg, William O. *A History of Habsburg Jews, 1670–191*. Bloomington: Indiana University Press, 1989.

Megargee, Geoffrey P., and Martin Dean, eds. *Encyclopedia of Camps and Ghettos*, vol. 2. Bloomington: University of Indiana Press, 2012.

Merck, Mandy. "The Train of Thought in Freud's 'Case of Homosexuality in a Woman.'" *m/f* 11–12 (1986): 35–46.

Mijolla-Mellor, Sophie de. "The Psychogenesis of a Case of Homosexuality in a Woman." *International Dictionary of Psychoanalysis Online*. New York: Macmillan Reference USA, 2005.

Oosterhuis, Harry. "Freud, and Albert Moll: How Kindred Spirits Became Bitter Foes." *History of Psychiatry* 31, no. 3 (2020): 294–310.

Oosterhuis, Harry. "Richard von Krafft-Ebing's 'Step-Children of Nature': Psychiatry and the Making of Homosexual Identity." In *Science and Homosexualities*, edited by Vernon A. Rosario. New York: Routledge, 1997.

Oosterhuis, Harry. "Sexual Modernity in the Works of Richard von Krafft-Ebing and Albert Moll." *Medical History* 56, no. 2 (April 2012): 133–155.

Oosterhuis, Harry. *Stepchildren of Nature: Krafft-Ebing, Psychiatry, and the Making of Sexual Identity*. Chicago: University of Chicago Press, 2000.

Ophuijsen, Johan H. W.Van "Contributions to the Masculinity Complex in Women." *International Journal of Psychoanalysis* 5 (1924): 39–49.

Prokop, Ursula. *Zum jüdischen Erbe in der Wiener Architektur. Der Beitrag jüdischer ArchitektInnen am Wiener Baugeschehen 1868–1938*. Vienna: Böhlau, 2016.

Reiter, Paul. *Bambi's Jewish Roots and Other Essays on German-Jewish Culture*. London: Bloomsbury, 2015.

Rieder, Ines, and Diana Voigt, eds. *The Story of Sidonie C.: Freud's Famous "Case of Female Homosexuality,"* translated by Jill Hannum and Ines Rieder. Budapest: Helena History Press, 2019.

Riviere, Joan. "Womanliness as Masquerade." *International Journal of Psychoanalysis* 10 (1929): 303–313.

Roof, Judith A. "Freud Reads Lesbians: The Male Homosexual Imperative." *Arizona Quarterly* 46, no. 1 (Spring 1990): 17–26.

Rose, Alison. *Jewish Women in Fin de Siècle Vienna.* Austin: University of Texas Press, 2008.

Rose, Jacqueline. *Sexuality in the Field of Vision.* New York: Verso, 1986.

Rozenblit, Marsha L. *The Jews of Vienna, 1867–1914: Assimilation and Identity.* Albany: State University of New York Press, 1983.

Sandgruber, Roman. *Traumzeit für Millionäre: Die 929 reichsten Wienerinnen und Wiener im Jahr 1910.* Vienna: Styria, 2013.

Sarnitz, August. *Otto Wagner.* New York: Taschen, 2018.

Sauerteig, Lutz D. H. "Loss of Innocence: Albert Moll, Sigmund Freud and the Invention of Childhood Sexuality Around 1900." *Medical History* 56, no. 2 (2012): 156–183.

Savoia, Paolo "Sexual Science and Self-Narrative: Epistemology and Narrative Technologies of the Self Between Krafft-Ebing and Freud." *History of the Human Sciences* 23, no. 5 (2010): 17–41.

Schorske, Carl E. *Fin-de-siècle Vienna.* New York: Vintage, 1980.

Schwaner, Birgit. *The Viennese Coffee House: Legend, Culture, Atmosphere.* Vienna: Pichler Verlag, 2007.

Sealey, Anne. "The Strange Case of the Freudian Case History: The Role of Long Case Histories in the Development of Psychoanalysis." *History of the Human Sciences* 24, no. 1 (2011): 36–50.

Shapira, Elana. *Style and Seduction: Jewish Patrons, Architecture, and Design in Fin de Siècle Vienna.* Waltham, MA: Brandeis University Press, 2016.

Shapira, Michal. "A Case for a 'Middle-Way Career,' in the History of Psychology: The Work of Pioneering Psychoanalyst Marjorie Brierley in Early 20th Century Britain." *History of Psychology* 24, no. 1 (2021): 55–76.

Shapira, Michal. "Criticizing Phallocentrism in Interwar Britain: Psychoanalyst Sylvia M. Payne's Kleinian Challenge to Freud." *Modern Intellectual History* (2021): 1–24.

Shapira, Michal. "Indecently Exposed: The Male Body and Vagrancy in Metropolitan London before the Fin de Siècle." *Gender & History* 30, no. 1 (March 2018): 52–69.

Shapira, Michal. "Not Unsympathetic: Freud's Lesser-Known 1920 Case of the Female Homosexuality of Margarethe Csonka." *Journal of the History of Sexuality* 32, no. 3 (October 2023): 340–374.

Shapira, Michal. "'Speaking Kleinian': Susan Isaacs as Ursula Wise and the Inter-War Popularisation of Psychoanalysis." *Medical History* 61, no. 4 (October 2017): 525–547.

Shapira, Michal. *The War Inside: Psychoanalysis, Total War, and the Making of the Democratic Self in Postwar Britain*. New York: Cambridge University Press, 2013.

Sigusch, Volkmar. "The Sexologist Albert Moll – Between Sigmund Freud and Magnus Hirschfeld." *Medical History* 56, no. 2 (2012): 184–200.

Simmel, Georg. "The Metropolis and Mental Life." In *The Blackwell City Reader*, edited by Gary Bridge and Sophie Watson, 103–110. Oxford: Wiley-Blackwell, 2010.

Smith, Jill Suzanne. *Berlin Coquette: Prostitution and the New German Woman, 1890–1933*. Ithaca, NY: Cornell University Press, 2003.

Smith-Rosenberg, Carol. *Disorderly Conduct: Visions of Gender in Victorian America*. New York: Oxford University Press, 1985.

Sulloway, Frank. *Freud, Biologist of the Mind: Beyond the Psychoanalytic Legend*. New York: Basic Books, 1979.

Sulloway, Frank J. "Reassessing Freud's Case Histories: The Social Construction of Psychoanalysis." *Isis* 82 (1991): 245–275.

Sutton, Katie. *Sex Between Body and Mind: Psychoanalysis and Sexology in the German-Speaking World, 1890s-1930s*. Ann Arbor: University of Michigan Press, 2020.

Tamagne, Florence. *History of Homosexuality in Europe: Berlin, London, Paris 1919–1939*. New York: Algora Publishing, 2003.

Topp, Leslie. *Architecture and Truth in Fin-de-Siècle Vienna*. Cambridge: Cambridge University Press, 2004.

Tzur-Mahalel, Anat. "'Are We Dead': Time in H.D.'s Dialogue with Freud." *International Journal of Psychoanalysis* 102, no. 2 (2021): 297–314.

Tzur-Mahalel, Anat. *Reading Freud's Patients: Memoir, Narrative, and the Analysand*. London and New York: Routledge, 2020.

Tzur-Mahalel, Anat. "The Wolf Man's Glückshaube: Rereading Sergei Pankejeff's Memoir." *Journal of the American Psychoanalytic Association* 67, no. 5 (2019): 789–813.

Vicinus, Martha. *Intimate Friends: Women Who Loved Women, 1778–1929*. Chicago: University of Chicago Press, 2004.

Vegesack, Alexander von. *Thonet: Classic Furniture in Bent Wood and Tubular Steel*. Rizzoli: New York, 1997.

Vyleta, Daniel M. *Crime, Jews and News: Vienna 1895–1914*. New York: Berghahn, 2007.

Walkowitz, Judith R. *City of Dreadful Delight: Narratives of Sexual Danger in Late- Victorian London*. Chicago: University of Chicago Press, 1992.

Walkowitz, Judith R. "Going Public: Shopping, Street Harassment, and Streetwalking in Late Victorian London." *Representations* 62 (1998): 1–30.

Waters, Chris. "Havelock Ellis, Sigmund Freud and the State: Discourses of Homosexual Identity in Interwar Britain." In *Sexology in Culture: Labelling Bodies and Desires*, edited by L. Bland and L. Doan. Chicago: University of Chicago Press, 1998.

Weeks, Jeffrey. *Coming Out: Homosexual Politics in Britain, from the Nineteenth Century to the Present*. London: Quartet Books, 1977.

Worthington, Anne. *Female Homosexuality: Psychoanalysis and Queer Theory*. PhD dissertation. London: Middlesex University, 2011.

Archives

Archiv der Erzdiözese Wien (Archive of the Archdiocese of Vienna).
Archiv der Israelitische Kultusgemeinde Wien (Vienna Jewish Community Archive).
Archiv der Stadt Budapest (Budapest City Archive).
Brandenburg Military Records, Berlin.
Evangelical Church Register Office, Hanover.
Freud Museum, London.
Freud Museum, Vienna.
Hungarian National Archives.
Landesarchiv Berlin (Berlin State Archive).
Library of Congress, Washington, DC, Sigmund Freud and Kurt R. Eissler papers.
Österreichisches Staatsarchiv (Austrian State Archives).

Archival Databases/Websites

www.ancestry.com.
www.anno.onb.ac.at (operated by the Austrian National Library).
www.deutsche-digitale-bibliothek.de/newspaper (Deutsches Zeitungsportal, operated by the German National Library).
www.familysearch.org.
www.findagrave.com.
www.findbuch.at.
www.friedhoefewien.at.
www.genealogyindexer.org.
www.geschichtewiki.wien.gv.at.
www.jewishgen.org.
www.newspapers.com.
www.sammlung.wienmuseum.at.

Newspapers

Berliner Tageblatt, March 31, 1924, 3.
Die Neue Zeitung, April 24, 1924, 3.
Die Zeit, April 24, 1913, 3.
Montag mit dem Sport-Montag, March 31, 1924, 1–2.
Neues Wiener Journal, October 11, 1912, 8.
Salzburger Chronik, October 11, 1912, 5.
Salzburger Volksblatt, April 25, 1913, 11.
South Florida Sun Sentinel, November 26, 1995.
Wiener Salonblatt, December 24, 1921, 6.

Index

Flanders, Sara 7n10, 18–20, 51n30,
51n33, 52n46–52, 53n56, 59n160,
117
Fleig Frank, Alison 105n107,
117
Forrester, John 6n1, 9, 49n1, 49n5,
50n6, 50n8, 117
Franz, Karl 83–84
Freud Museum, Vienna xi, xii,
63–64, 98n2, 112–113
Freud, Anna 6n3
Freud, Sigmund (works): "Analysis
of a Phobia in a Five-Year-Old
Boy" (Little Hans, 1909) 1, 10,
50n11, 52n50, 117; "Female
Sexuality" 52n54, 54n76, 58n143,
58n146; "Fragment of an Analysis
of a Case of Hysteria" (Dora,
1905) 1, 10, 50n9, 118; "From the
History of an Infantile Neurosis"
(Wolf Man, 1918) 1, 10, 50n13,
118; "Leonardo da Vinci and a
Memory of his Childhood" 44,
52n51; "Letter to an American
Mother" 20, 53n57, 118; "Notes
upon a Case of Obsessional
Neurosis" (Rat Man, 1909) 1, 10,
50n10, 118; "On Narcissism: An
Introduction" 52n52, 118;
"Psycho-Analytic Notes on an
Autobiographical Account of a
Case of Paranoia (Dementia
Paranoides)" (Daniel Paul
Schreber, 1911) 1, 10, 50n12,
52n53, 60n165, 118; "The
Psychogenesis of a Case of
Homosexuality in a Woman"
(1920) 1–3, 6n1, 6n2, 6n3, 12–14,
19, 20–24, 25, 35, 38–39, 40,
41–43, 44, 45–48, 51n22, 52n49,
58n145, 61, 80–82, 92, 97, 98n3,
101n51, 108, 118; "The
Psychogenesis of a Case of Female
Homosexuality" 6n3, 118; "Some
Neurotic Mechanisms in Jealousy,
Paranoia and Homosexuality"
52n53, 118; "Some Psychical
Consequences of the Anatomical
Distinction between the Sexes"
52n48, 54n76, 118; "Three Essays

on the Theory of Sexuality" (1905)
3, 14–21, 36–37, 40, 42, 43, 44,
49n3, 51n29, 56n110, 118
Frosh, Steven 48, 60n179, 106n115,
118
Fuss, Diana 1, 5n1, 60n162, 98n3,
118

Galicia 77, 90, 91
Gay, Peter 31, 51n26, 54n72,
54n79,114n1, 119
German Penal Code Paragraph 175
26, 31, 36
German Empire 25, 26
Nazi Germany 111
Germany's invasion of Austria
111
Gessman, Albert (Jr.) 112–113,
115n6, 115n7
Gilman, Sander L. 48, 51n29, 54n62,
60n180, 60n183, 119
Goldstein, Jan 51n21, 119
Gothaisches genealogisches
Taschenbuch der gräflichen
Häuser 103n76, 119
Graf, Max 98n4, 99n7, 119
Grand Hotel Panhans, Location 62,
98n5
Grigg, Russell 66n177, 119
Gronberg, Tag 99n9, 119
Grosskurth, Phyllis 58n150, 119
Grosz, Elizabeth 2, 6n1, 7n11, 114n1,
119

Hamer, Diane 6n1, 119
Hanover 26
hate 22, 97
hermaphroditism 17, 20, 41, 43
Herzog, Dagmar 7n7, 53n57,
59n162, 60n170, 60n182, 119
heterosexual masculinity 23
history of sexuality 2, 4, 17
Hoffmann, Josef 71, 72
Holocaust 105n104, 114
Holnstein, Karl von 84, 103n76
homophobia 5, 21, 46, 49, 109
Hungarian National Archives
105n103, 105n105
hysteria 3, 8n21, 14, 21, 32, 46, 48,
49

For Product Safety Concerns and Information please contact our EU
representative GPSR@taylorandfrancis.com
Taylor & Francis Verlag GmbH, Kaufingerstraße 24, 80331 München, Germany

www.ingramcontent.com/pod-product-compliance
Lightning Source LLC
Chambersburg PA
CBHW050614280326
41932CB00016B/3043